Cartier

CREATIVE WRITING

Cartier

CREATIVE WRITING

François Chaille

photography by **Noëlle Hoeppe**

translated from the French by **Deke Dusinberre**

Flammarion

Paris·New York

CONCEPT
Franco Cologni

EDITORIAL DIRECTION
Suzanne Tise-Isoré

DESIGN AND ART DIRECTION
Bernard Lagacé
Compagnie Bernard Baissait, Paris

EDITING
Bernard Wooding

PROJECT DIRECTOR
Michel Aliaga

PHOTOENGRAVING
Arti Crom, Italy

PRINTING AND BINDING
Gajani, Italy

Published simultaneously in French by Flammarion
under the title *Cartier Styles et Stylos,* and in
Italien under the title *Styles et Stylos: Le penne di Cartier*

Flammarion
26 rue Racine
75006 Paris

ISBN: 2-0801-3683-6
Numéro d'édition: FA 368301
Dépôt légal: October 2000
Printed in Italy

Contents

If Cartier has been known worldwide as the "king of jewelers" and the "jeweler of kings" for over 150 years, that is because the company symbolizes everything that is most magnificent in the sphere of gems. By the early twentieth century, Cartier was official supplier to royal courts and high aristocrats. Asian monarchs (such as the king of Siam), maharajahs, czars, grand dukes, and the kings of Spain and England rubbed elbows with the richest bankers and industrial magnates in Cartier boutiques in Paris, London, and New York. Louis and his brothers Pierre and Jacques, grandsons of founder Louis-François Cartier, headed the firm in the early part of the twentieth century, transforming it into an abiding legend. In the minds of all, Cartier was a temple of fabulous marvels whose magnificence could be imagined from the sparkle of wonderful gems actually glimpsed in the shop window. Everyone knew, for instance, that Her Majesty the Queen of Spain, Victoria Eugenia, was not content with what was displayed for mere passersby. Thus a small crowd of curious onlookers waited outside the store on 13 rue de la Paix in Paris, where she had been seen entering, perhaps trying to imagine the extraordinary jewelry she would select or order, certainly hoping to see a reflection of it in her eyes when she finally came out. That incident occurred in 1925. But it might also have happened during a visit—as many photos testify—by the king of Sweden or the queens of Greece, Romania, and elsewhere. A stop at Cartier's was an essential part of any trip to Paris, London, or New York by a crowned head. Glittering tiaras of pearls and diamonds, heavy necklaces of emeralds and sapphires, gems as legendary as the "Jubilee" diamond (245 carats) and the "Queen of Holland" diamond (136 carats), a necklace of three strands of pink pearls, and countless other wonders passed through the hands of the "jeweler to kings." In the latter half of the century, the Cartier legend survived

The hand-worked nib of the **platinum-finish**

Louis Cartier pen.

intact because its workshops still designed or set the finest of gems, such as the fabulous emerald necklace designed for Barbara Hutton in 1947, the panther items made for Princess Nina Aga Khan from 1957 to 1960, and the 69-carat drop diamond that Richard Burton offered Elizabeth Taylor in 1969. Only Cartier's extreme discretion concerning current clients makes it impossible to follow this trail into the present.

The Cartier legend was therefore built in the marvelous shimmer of gems and precious metals, transformed into magnificent finery by the unrivaled skills of "house" artisans. Yet if Cartier is now synonymous with perfection, that is also due to the wonderful accessories it has always offered, both functional and decorative. Its watches, clocks, chests, vanity cases, mirrors, and cigarette holders have been crafted from precious materials, often set with gems of great value, always designed with refinement and unbelievable ingenuity. Ever since the 1860s, writing implements have numbered among these items—pen holders of jasper or platinum, dip pens in gold or tortoiseshell set with diamonds, mechanical pencils decorated in enamel or set with a cabochon, inkwells of agate or pink crystal, and so on. Although functional, such objects were no less precious than jewelry. Now that the concept of luxury has considerably changed, evolving from the thrill of priceless objects to the serene sensuality of timeless ones, writing instruments represent another chapter in the Cartier legend, whether richly decorated or quite simply of rare elegance and impeccable quality. That is because fine pens and pencils now offer a pleasure which is irrevocably denied to modern keyboard tools: the luxury of an age-old experience, of performing a natural yet magical act, of enjoying a sensual intimacy with materials and forms crafted with exceptional skill. Such implements are therefore worthy of the veritable rite

RIGHT: A design for the late 1920s: a silver paper knife with lapis-lazuli handle set with cabochon turquoises. Cartier Archives. FOLLOWING PAGES: Selection of finely worked **gold pen nibs** currently produced by Cartier. Thirty-six different models exist in five writing widths.

of writing by hand. It would be tragic to lose the ritual of tracing letters in ink on paper by a hand that obeys a mind fully concentrated upon that task, to the more or less scratchy sound of a nib. Contrary to uniquely functional—and often disposable—pens which deprive the act of writing of all symbolic value, handsome Cartier implements magnify that moment, sanctifying it. They themselves are very special, the result of a lengthy and loving creative process. They thereby spur fine writing—the drawing of fine letters, the crafting of fine phrases, perhaps even inspiring fine ideas. By offering accessories that are both beautiful and technologically perfect to aficionados of handwriting, by making these items one of its most fertile fields of creativity, Cartier renewed and transcended the prestigious calling it has followed from the start: to dazzle the eye with the beautiful, the rare, and the timeless, here placed at the service of writing, one of humankind's most noble activities.

CHAPTER I

Five Thousand Years

of Writing

The great civilizations emerged alongside writing some five thousand years ago, and no objects invented by humans are richer in historical and symbolic meaning than the implements with which they write: "Tell me what you write with, I'll tell you who you are." This technological adage was joined by another, more psychological one in the nineteenth century: "Tell me *how* you write . . ."

Fashioning tools for writing—for leaving a permanent trace—is what characterizes a society able to master its history. Able to preserve ancient knowledge, to pass it on, to insure its future. Able to remember beyond individual memories, able to imagine beyond personal horizons, able to measure beyond private landmarks. And also able to listen to the sacred words of gods, to communicate silently, to speak in secret, to reach distant ears. Along with agriculture, writing was the one major invention that enabled mankind to acquire the magic powers which turned people into civilized beings forever. In other words, it made them powerful and relatively independent of the laws of nature—for better or for worse.

The ability to create beauty probably remains the most admirable of mankind's magic powers. Art arose before writing, of course, and today's painters should perhaps dwell more often on the wonderful technique, refinement, descriptive vitality, and unsurpassable enchantment of images that naked—and probably savage—men drew with their hands on the walls of caves. It seems as though the entire art of painting came from heaven along with the gift of life. The problem is that men of that time were savage and naked, much closer to animals than to the *Homo sapiens* we have become today. Their sublime art sprang from a survival instinct—it was meant to ward off fear, to call down mysterious powers. It was just another tool, like a sharpened flint or a club. Often totally invisible in the blackness of a cave, art existed for a sake other than its own.

The art of *Homo sapiens*, in contrast, which had no purpose other than generating pleasure and feelings, emerged more or less at the same time as writing. It evoked the sensual pleasure and special emotion of beholding beauty (whatever is meant by that word, the most relative in the human vocabulary). The earliest examples of "art for art's sake" (as Romantics and symbolists would later proclaim) were probably religious in origin. In Egypt, where the first complete writing system was developed, the decoration of

PRECEDING PAGE: **Chinese painted scrolls,**
19th century, private collection. RIGHT: Design for a **dip pen** (circa 1925) of gold, jade, nephrite, and rubies. Pencil, gouache, and watercolor on tracing paper, 18.1 x 2.1 cm. Cartier Archives.

tombs and especially temples had to fulfill meticulous religious requirements. Yet in attempting to depict the totality of the living world so that the deceased could take it into the afterlife, painters could not prevent themselves from instilling their designs—even as they respected strict codes—with a very special and very human emotion. Whether arising from a clutch of lotus flowers or from the suggestion of a woman's body beneath a garment, it was this emotion that would be the deceased's most valued resource in the subterranean world of the dead.

Egypt was also the cradle of pure art, however. No priest obliged people to build splendidly elegant furniture for noblemen, or to fashion dazzling jewels for their wives, yet everyday objects were designed to be both functional and beautiful. Mirrors, containers for precious ointments and make-up, flasks of scented oil, chests, precious crockery, vases—everything that the great Egyptologist Émile Prisse d'Avennes dubbed "industrial art"—sprang from the workshops of incredibly skilled craftsmen who achieved supreme refinement. And of course artisans also crafted the tools of the revolution wrought by scholars, namely writing instruments. For at least four of the five thousand years that such implements have existed, people have wanted them to be as beautiful as they were useful.

⌘

By putting his jeweler's talent at the service of writing implements in the 1860s, Louis-François Cartier thus adopted a tradition thousands of years old. Two entries in a venerable Cartier sales ledger, kept for nearly a century, take us back in time—via the imagination—to the ancient Egyptian origins of that tradition. One entry is dated May 5, 1904, and notes the purchase of a mechanical pencil in fluted white gold, set with a cabochon sapphire. The other entry, dated December 18, 1905, concerns the purchase of two items: a dip pen in enamel and blond tortoiseshell, gilded with laurel, and a matching pen stand. These three refined objects were chosen by Lady Almina Carnarvon, the young wife of a man who would leave his mark on the history of Egyptology: George Edward Stanhope Molyneux Herbert, fifth earl of Carnarvon. Almina and George Carnarvon were regulars at the shop on boulevard des Italiens (and later on rue de la Paix when Cartier moved there in 1899). The pretty countess had bought several jewelry

pieces, while the earl acquired, among other things, a cigarette case and a cane knob in pink enamel. Prior to the years 1904 and 1905, however, neither had bought pen or pencil. This interest in writing accessories was perhaps triggered by the intense impressions of Lady Carnarvon during a 1903 trip to the land of the earliest scribes, an initiatory journey that would be followed by many others. The couple, married for eight years at the time, was about to develop an extraordinary passion for ancient Egypt. This passion drove them to finance the excavations of Howard Carter for twenty years, leading to the discovery of Tutankhamun's tomb. That tomb contained, among other marvels, wonderful writing objects that either belonged to the pharaoh or were simply precious doubles of everyday objects, specially designed for the eternal scribe Amun-Re, whom every pharaoh became upon his death. Carter inventoried fourteen scribe's palettes; such palettes were normally simple tablets of wood or schist, hollowed out to contain a few sharpened reeds and two pans of ink (red and black), but these royal palettes were of finely carved ivory or gilded, precious wood. One of them stood out as an exceptional piece: some twelve inches long, in carved ivory partially covered with gold leaf, it still contained seven reeds and the remains of two little pans of red and black ink. It bore the pharaoh's name, "Beloved of the gods Atum, Amun-Re and Thoth," and it might be supposed that Tutankhamun actually used it. Carter also discovered two ink pans made of horn, an extraordinary, finely worked gilded wood case for reeds, a gold and ivory papyrus smoother bearing a dedication to Thoth, god of scribes, a small piece of polished sandstone that served as eraser, and a box for papyrus (empty, alas), not to mention painting palettes and colors, and a wonderful water cup in red-tinted ivory.

Egyptian art inspired Cartier as early as the 1850s, when bracelets, brooches, and earrings were based on motifs discovered in the Nile Valley. This **vanity case** of enameled gold, coral, lapis lazuli, emeralds, and diamonds on platinum, dating from 1927, employs two carved calcite plaque fragments formerly on an amulet made around 500 B.C.E., depicting Horus on one side and a magical incantation on the other. Between 1910 and the late 1930s, Cartier produced an impressive array of objects that incorporated Egyptian antiquities. Art de Cartier Collection. LEFT: An **Egyptian Temple Gate Clock** (1927) featuring mock hieroglyphs, in mother of pearl, coral, enameled gold, and lapis lazuli. Art de Cartier Collection.

By the time Tutankhamun briefly reigned among the living, humans along the Nile had been writing for two thousand years. Writing already boasted a long history, a vibrant antiquity. Hieroglyphic writing was thoroughly alive yet frozen, since it had not changed for two thousand years and would not change for nearly another two millennia, at which point it suddenly vanished forever. Throughout all that immutable time—that eternity—certain children of the Nile, those chosen by birth, learned to draw hieroglyphs on papyrus. Their difficult apprenticeship began at age ten: first they learned how to cut

papyrus with the aid of a knife and smooth it with a plank; they practiced holding and unrolling it with the left hand while the right rolled it up again. They were taught to prepare reed pens: the tip of the reed, gathered along the banks of the Nile, was split and sharpened into a point (or, to the contrary, flattened, depending on the width desired). And they had to know how to make inks: powdered soot and water mixed with a little gum arabic for black ink (used for ordinary text), powdered cinnabar or red lead for red ink (for titles and chapter heads). Above all, they learned how to draw several thousand hieroglyphs thanks to copying and dictation exercises—and blows from the master's cane. They were also taught to erase mistakes with a polished stone or scrape them with a blade without tearing the papyrus so that it might be used again. For papyrus was a costly affair, and could not be wasted. The state had a monopoly on its manufacture; specialized civil servants thus made mankind's earliest "sheets," harvesting the stems of the plant and converting them into long, thin strands that could be woven together and superimposed in layers. Then the sheets would have to be dried, polished, softened, and glued together into a scroll of several sheets.

Hieroglyphs, the first writing system that made it possible to express things with all the subtlety required of both divine speech and human literature, were nevertheless preceded by another, much more primitive, system. Ancient clay tablets discovered in the city of Uruk in lower Mesopotamia, dating from a century or two before the earliest hieroglyphs, were engraved with pictographic symbols. Invented in the fourth millennium B.C.E. (and sufficiently developed over the centuries to be able to recount the famous tale of *Gilgamesh*), these primitive pictographs were pressed into soft clay with the aid of a reed stylus. Every sign depicted the shape or symbol of the thing it referred to, and the oldest tablets so far recovered are merely small ledgers—accounts of livestock or measures of harvests. Later, Sumerian scribes sharpened their reeds in order to make wedge-shaped marks which, depending on their direction, represented a stylized form of the original figure. Such writing has since been labeled "cuneiform," from the Latin *cuneus*, "wedge." Little by little, cuneiform incorporated phonetic symbols and became the writing system used by Babylonians and Assyrians as well. Functional and sophisticated, cuneiform was ultimately able to transcribe languages other than the Sumerian and

Ivory **scribe's palettes** from the tomb of Tutankhamun (18th dynasty). The larger palette (30 cm) still contains seven reeds, while the smaller one bears traces of pigment. LEFT: **Tomb painting** showing three scribes of Pharaoh Tuthmosis IV (18th dynasty, Luxor).

Akkadian of its birth—the Hittites, for example, adopted it for their own Indo-European language. The Hittites, originally from Anatolia, not only developed a civilization that reached its pinnacle between the fifteenth and thirteenth centuries B.C.E., but were also avid letter-writers. The oldest surviving letters in history are Hittite, written some four thousand years ago in cuneiform on clay tablets, themselves placed in clay envelopes marked with the recipient's address: business letters, private letters to the family, and feverish love letters written with the tip of a reed.

One of these letters takes us back to Egypt. The Hittite king Suppiluliumas wrote to the pharaoh Amenophis IV—later known as the heretic Akhenaton—to shower him with blessings on his accession to the throne in the fourteenth century B.C.E. In Egypt, scribes had ingeniously developed, very early on, a writing derived from hieroglyphs, which they used for everyday business. Called hieratic, this flowing, cursive style was easier and faster to write. Also unearthed in Egypt were the oldest traces of one of writing's most startling inventions: the alphabet. In an alphabet, symbols no longer refer to things, but rather to sounds. And since there are far fewer sounds in a language than there are things in the world, two or three dozen symbols suffice to transcribe everything. Strangely, this invention was not Egyptian—the ancient Egyptians themselves never used any system other than hieroglyphs and its various cursive derivatives (excepting their late adoption of Greek). Yet it was in Egypt, at Wadi el-Hol, on rocks along the trail leading from Thebes to the oases of the Western Desert, that the oldest alphabetic text in the world can be seen, dating from 1800 B.C.E. This text has not yet been deciphered, but would seem to involve a Semitic language similar to Akkadian. It was probably carved on stone by foreign traders or Semitic mercenaries in the Egyptian army. Specialists are still divided over the nature of this writing, only discovered in the late 1990s: is it a simplification of hieroglyphs, and therefore a transitional form of writing halfway between the Egyptian system and the Phoenician alphabet, from which almost all the world's alphabets have descended? If such is the case, Semitic immigrants into Egypt were probably the inventors of the alphabet. Or is it merely the oldest trace of a Semitic alphabet called Proto-Sinaitic, completely unrelated to hieroglyphs, whose use was later attested among populations in the Sinai? Along with the Ugaritic alphabet that emerged around the fifteenth century

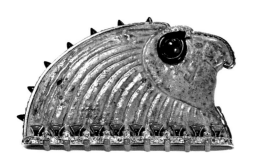

Egyptian blue-glazed faience **Horus Head Brooch** (1925) in platinum, yellow gold, coral, onyx and diamonds, with cabochon emerald eye. Art de Cartier Collection. RIGHT: Detail of a fourth-century B.C.E. **sarcophagus cover**, decorated with hieroglyphs in pâte de verre. Hieroglyphs, invented some 5,000 years ago, represented the first sophisticated system of writing.

Ceramic **recipients** used by Chinese calligraphers

in the sixteenth century. Ancient Chinese writing dates

back three thousand years and is the oldest still in use.

B.C.E. on the coast of what is now Syria, the Proto-Sinaitic alphabet was a precursor of the Phoenician alphabet.

❧

Humanity's first writing implements, then, were reeds (for tracing ink on papyrus or marking soft clay), knives or chisels (for carving stone). The use of reeds long survived in the hands of Arab calligraphers attempting to trace letters so beautiful they would be worthy of the word of God, sometimes forming sophisticated picture-poems. Another instrument from antiquity has also survived, doggedly composing the oldest writing in the world for at least three and a half millennia: namely, the brush used to write Chinese, still employed by a few calligraphers. Of course, the earliest traces of this writing—oracular inscriptions—were engraved with a sharp point on the shoulder blades of deer or the shells of tortoises. But Chinese calligraphy enjoyed a first blossoming during the Han dynasty in the second century B.C.E., then in the fifth century became a Buddhist art of brush and (indelible) ink that reflected a person's total being. The finest Chinese brushes were veritable works of art with handles of jade, ivory or porcelain. Other ancient instruments did not enjoy that status, notably the simple metal styluses used by the Greeks and Roman to mark wax-coated tablets of wood or ivory, a technique probably invented by the Hittites. One side of the stylus was sharp for marking, while the other was blunt for erasing mistakes. This system was ingenious but fleeting, since in the West a new, unbeatable implement was about to reign for a millennium—the quill pen, made from bird feathers.

The rise of quills owed everything to the invention of a new surface to write on, one that was stronger, cheaper, and more convenient than papyrus—namely, parchment. Although animal skins had been used from time to time as a writing surface back in antiquity, parchment was allegedly developed in Pergamum in Asia Minor (its name being derived from the Greek for "[stuff] from Pergamum"). In the second century B.C.E., Ptolemy Epiphanes in Alexandria, jealous of the mounting reputation of the library of his Attalid rivals, reportedly decreed an embargo on the export of papyrus to Pergamum. The city's craftsmen then apparently perfected parchment by using the skin of sheep, calf, or goat. The skins were first of all cleaned with quicklime and all the fur and fat were carefully

An **inkwell** (1930) in steatite with a Chinese calligraphic seal on the lid, trimmed with gold and black lacquer fillets. The ebonite base is decorated with red lacquer reeding. Cartier Archives. FOLLOWING PAGES: A few of Cartier's **chinoiseries**: a crystal pen and pencil set with crystal base (1930), and an inkwell in jade, enamel, coral, and nephrite (1929). Cartier Archives.

removed. Then they were scraped, dried, thinned, polished with a pumice stone, and finally cut into sheets. The very fine and supple skin of new-born calves yielded the luxurious "vellum." In the Mediterranean area, parchment only really began to rival papyrus in the fourth century, and the latter continued to be made in Egypt and Sicily until the tenth century. By that time, however, all medieval Europe was writing on parchment, whether fashioned into a scroll or into a codex, that is to say sheets folded and bound together into a book.

Softer and more absorbent than papyrus, parchment permitted the use of a more flexible—and therefore more accurate—implement than reed or stylus, namely the wing feather of a bird such as duck, rooster, eagle or raven. Goose quills, in particular, were not only easy to come by but were especially long and supple, felt good in the hand, and were not too difficult to sharpen. Since a quill would wear down quickly, it had to be regularly sharpened according to precise methods to produce the desired style of writing. One of the first treatises on the art of sharpening quills (along with those of making ink and forming letters) was the famous *Libro nuovo d'imparare a scrivere*, published in Italy in 1540 by Giovanni Battista Palatino (whose name was given to a font well-known to typesetters and word-processor users). A quill had to be sharpened with the help of a special, small knife—the "pen-knife." The hollow tip was cut on a diagonal and a small slit

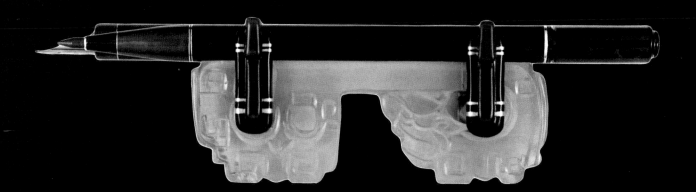

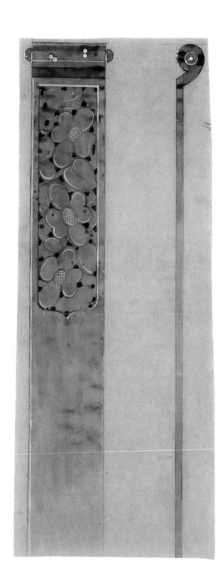

was made up the middle, then it was shaped into a nib. Every pen and style of writing called for a special cut. In the eighteenth century, the entry for "Art of Writing" in Diderot's *Encyclopédie* provided crucial advice in this respect and conveyed the level of refinement and subtlety attained by the art of writing at that time: "The quill is sharpened broad or narrow depending on the strength of character to be shaped, and depending on the nature of that character. For round, composed penmanship—large, average, or small—it must be split a little less than two lines deep, cut away at the level of the slit, and hollowed below the two edges separating the main cut from the tip of the quill, in such manner that the point of the pen is the [same] length as the slit . . . For a *bastarda* style, the slit should be roughly two lines deep, or a little longer than for round [hand-writing] . . . For a running hand—large, average, or small—and for long strokes of the round and *bastarda* styles, the slit should be up to three lines deep, and the sides almost straight." However it was sharpened, a goose quill offered something not possible with a reed, something that would remain standard for letters traced by schoolchildren right up to the 1960s: the elegant combination of thick downstrokes (made by pressing firmly on the tip) and thin upstrokes (made with the edge). Also incorporated into this combination was the grace of drawing and the dance of the hand.

To simplify the task of sharpening, "mechanical sharpeners" and "pen recutters" appeared in the eighteenth century. Yet no sharpening, however perfect, could compensate for a poor-quality quill. The first job of any public scribe, clerk, copyist or letter-writer, then, was to choose the right one. In the "Quill Pen" entry of his *Encyclopédie*, Diderot himself offered some advice: "It should be round, truly clean and clear, as though transparent, without any sign of white blotches, which normally prevent it from splitting cleanly and cause small flakes to leave the body of the shaft from within . . . Many people prefer wing tips over all other feathers, because they normally split more cleanly. This is the reason that master Writers and their pupils are most satisfied with them."

In the days of goose quills, the labor of writing required many accessories in addition to feather and pen-knife. A medieval monk at his writing desk in the scriptorium, sometimes standing for hours at a stretch, flattened the sheet of his codex with a thin baton held in the left hand. He would then choose a quill from his case and dip it into

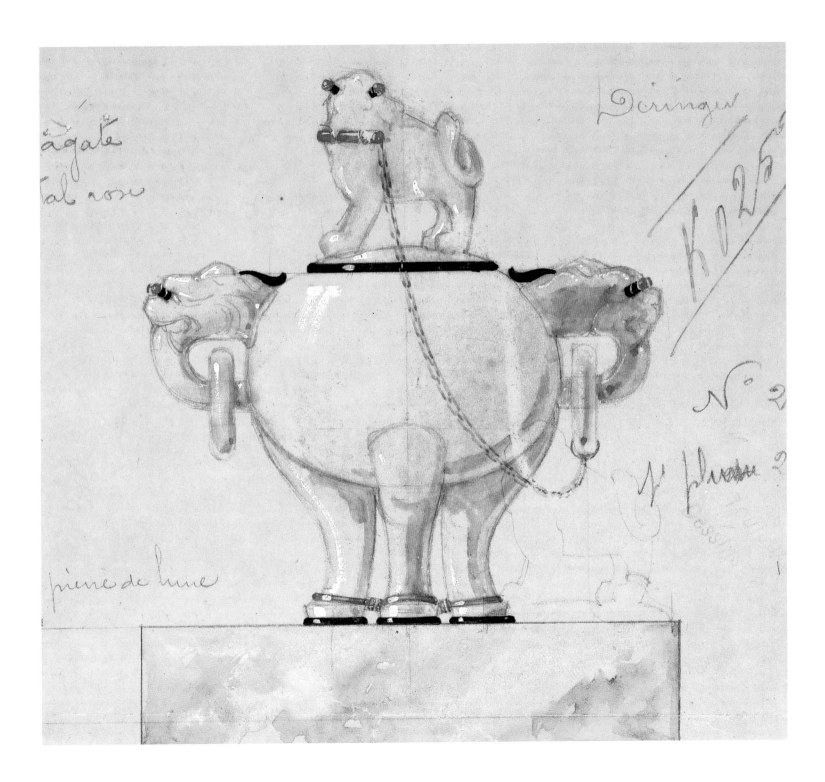

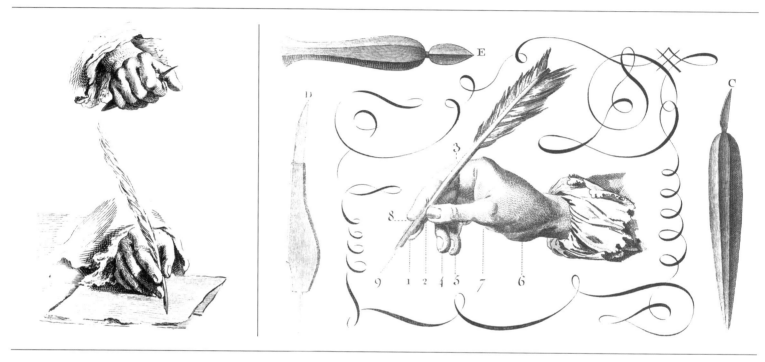

one of his inkwells. The ink would then be dusted with powder from a box, while mistakes could be erased with a scraper. Parchment could be scraped and written over several times; today's electronic equipment makes it possible to read the original texts beneath these palimpsests, which sometimes turn out to be long-lost works by "pagan" authors such as Ovid and Cicero.

As the extent of secular writing increased, the profession of "public scribe"—sometimes itinerant—gave birth to writing cases of leather or wood worn on the belt, containing the entire kit plus a seal and wax. Starting in the seventeenth century, goldsmiths, ceramists, and cutlers designed splendid ivory or horn pen-shafts (to hold nibs of chased silver), richly decorated pen cases, inkwells of fine porcelain, and ivory-handled penknives for the aristocracy. Writing—in particular of love letters—enjoyed unprecedented popularity among the educated in the eighteenth century.

People no longer wrote on parchment. By that time paper made from hemp or linen was common, having been invented by the Chinese at the dawn of the Christian era, adopted by the Arabs in the eighth century, and introduced into the West in the twelfth.

Light, supple, thin, foldable, and affordable, paper conquered a market in full expansion following the invention of printing. Even though pencils were used for drawing, thanks to the discovery of graphite deposits in Germany and England, a goose quill and ink were still used for writing. The scratching of pens on rag paper was the most commonly heard music of the Enlightenment. It resounded so loudly in private studies that sometimes it hindered the inspiration of poets and philosophers summoned by their muse in the middle of the night. "It often happened," wrote Goethe in *Poetry and Truth*, "that I would recite to myself a little piece of verse without being able to work it out, and sometimes I would rush to my desk and, without taking the time to straighten a sheet placed askew, without moving from there, I would write the poem from beginning to end, in a stroke. Along the same lines, I chose by preference a pencil, whose strokes were gentler, because it sometimes happened that the screeching and scratching of the pen awoke me, distracting me and smothering my tiny production at birth."

This scratching sound was not the only drawback of the most elegant writing implement ever invented. Frequent shortages, susceptibility to dampness (which softened it), and rapid wear on a tip that required regular but not always successful sharpening spurred writers to seek the ideal pen, that is to say a stable and hard-wearing one. All that was required were improvements to an already ancient device—the metal nib—which had been plagued by serious drawbacks. Starting in the sixteenth century, pens of sheet iron, brass, steel, copper, silver or gold began appearing all across Europe. But prior to 1820, all these pens were overly rigid, liable to rust, and above all costly. None of these efforts led to mass production or any serious competition to quills. It took the genius of a Birmingham craftsman, Joseph Gillot, to solve the remaining problems. In charge of splitting nibs in a metal-pen workshop, Gillot realized the considerable cost savings to be made if industrial methods were used. He therefore designed an industrial tool die for stamping pen nibs. A steel nib made this way cost one hundred times less than a hand-crafted one. Within twenty years, Gillot and other manufacturers such as Mitchell, Perry, and Mason made Birmingham the world capital of pens—they were inexpensive, almost never wore out, and were flexible enough to write as well as a quill. It was from that moment that Victor Hugo lamented the disappearance of fine old quills endowed with

Woman Sealing a Letter (detail) by Jean-Siméon Chardin (1699–1779). Stiftung Preussische Schlösser und Gärten, Schloss Charlottenberg, Berlin.

"the lightness of a breeze and the power of a thunderbolt," recalling that they had originally "taken wing and had flown."

But how could goose quills have survived a century of industrial revolution, how could they have met the enormous new demands for writing equipment? How could they have kept up with the terrific expansion of administrations, postal services, and schools? Cheap little steel nibs, produced in the billions and stuck into holders, would fulfill those needs wonderfully. And they would eventually give birth to fountain pens. Both dip pens and fountain pens provided the intense pleasure of handwriting finally freed from overly constraining codes. The pleasure is that of personal expression with a fine pen and fine paper, setting down marks as creative as the strokes of a painter's brush or a sculptor's chisel. This sensual pleasure probably dates back to primeval times—a very archaic drive to make a mark, already visible in prehistoric caves, as analyzed by Roland Barthes in his preface to Roger Druet's *La Civilisation de l'écriture*: "The human desire to incise (by needle, reed, stylus, pen) or caress (with brush or felt-tip) has perhaps undergone multiple metamorphoses that have occulted the truly bodily origins of writing; but it merely takes a painter every now and then (such as André Masson or Cy Twombly today) to incorporate graphic forms into his oeuvre for us to be reminded of this obvious fact—writing is not merely a technical activity, it is also a blissful bodily experience." Without overlooking technique, it is above all this blissful experience that Cartier defends and promotes through its outstanding writing tools. Simultaneously beautiful and sensual, they are entirely devoted to a pleasure that has existed from time immemorial.

A jeweler's great artistry is placed in the service of writing instruments—these five implements demonstrate Cartier's creative use of materials and color.

LEFT TO RIGHT: a gold **fountain pen** with coral band (1938, see p. 121); a traditional **dip pen** of agate and coral (1929, see p. 79); a gold **ballpoint** with bamboo motif (circa 1970, see p. 105); a gold **mechanical pencil** with lattice pattern of rose-cut diamonds (1947, see p. 125); a **mechanical pencil** in pink enamel on gold, with diamond push-rod (1906, see p. 63).

CHAPTER II

The Belle Époque
and Bejeweled Pens

Paris, Friday, October 27, 1876: the grand boulevards gave off the familiar scent of horse manure as a hackney carriage pulled up to the door of a shop at number 9 boulevard des Italiens. Ever since the nearby Opera House had been inaugurated some two years earlier, the neighborhood with its theaters and cafés had become even more fashionable. Women with cumbersome crinolines and frock-coated men in silly top hats (dubbed "stovepipes") strolled along, on the alert for novelty, the unexpected, the latest rumor. Passersby probably recognized the middle-aged woman, imposing of appearance and elegant of dress, who stepped down from the carriage and disappeared through the elegant doorway. The jeweler Louis-François Cartier, in business on this spot since 1869, had been supplier to several members of the imperial court, including the empress herself. Louis-François's son, Alfred, who had taken over the business two years earlier at the age of thirty-five, was still supplier to princely houses all over Europe—notably the imperial court of Russia—as well as to the affluent bourgeoisie of the young French republic. On that Friday, the woman who entered Cartier's plush wood-and-marble shop was none other than Princess Mathilde, niece of the first Napoleon and cousin of the recently deposed emperor. At fifty-six years old, she was no longer one of the most influential women of the Second Empire that had pathetically crumbled six years before. The princess nevertheless still reigned over literary and artistic Paris. She held salons every Wednesday evening for writers and every Thursday evening for painters, and every Sunday she gave a grand reception or ball.

Alfred greeted the princess like a friend. She had been a client for twenty years and always managed to establish friendly, straightforward relationships with the artists she liked. Louis-François and his son were among them, having designed for her a number of cameos, brooches, a magnificent pearl and ruby necklace, and dozens of other items of jewelry, not to mention various objects such as a parasol. On this day, however, Princess Mathilde wanted Alfred to show her objects of a type he had never sold to her. They still figure on the firm's old ledgers, which preserve the record of over 200 purchases concerning the princess, taking into account items ordered for her by one or another of her friends and lovers, such as Comte Alfred-Émilien de Nieuwekerque, for example, a sculptor in the service of the Empire who bought the princess her first Cartier jewelry in the 1850s.

Boulevard des Italiens in Paris, where Cartier was located from 1859 to 1899 (seen here circa 1900).

PRECEDING PAGE: A Cartier **dip pen** of 1907 (see p. 49).

The 1850s had been the years of her supreme splendor. This young, rich, dazzling cousin of Napoleon III had just freed herself from a bad marriage and had overcome several ordeals. Mathilde was the daughter of Jérôme Bonaparte—banished from France—and Catherine de Württemberg, and had grown up both in Rome—where her great-uncle, the grand collector Cardinal Fesch, initiated her into art appreciation—and in Florence, where her taste was honed by frequent visits to the Uffizi Gallery and the Palazzo Pitti. As a young girl, the princess began to draw and paint, activities she pursued throughout her life. She dreamed of collecting works and becoming an art patron like the Medicis, the Rucellais, and the Pittis. But how? The Bonapartes had lost everything, and she had been living in straitened circumstances ever since the premature death of her mother, who had benefited from a few stipends from her grandfather, the king of Württemberg. An answer appeared when, at age sixteen, it was thought that Mathilde

Princess Mathilde in her Studio, circa 1855, by Charles
Giraud. Musée du Château de Compiègne.
The Cartier archives record over two hundred purchases
by Princess Mathilde, cousin of Napoleon III.
Sometime around 1850, she became the firm's first
client from a ruling royal family. Her purchases included
two combination pens and mechanical pencils.

might marry her kind cousin, Louis-Napoleon, son of Louis Bonaparte (former king of
Holland) and Hortense de Beauharnais. Hortense, however, was concerned about the
financial situation of Mathilde's father, Jérôme, and the plan never materialized. Four
years later, all worries vanished when the princess agreed to marry a suitor, Anatole
Demidoff, whose vast fortune pleased her father enormously. Demidoff, the richest man
in Russia after the czar, owned colossal mines in the Urals and was styled the "Prince of
San Donato" on the strength of his bank account, but he was also an alcoholic brute. The
marriage was a disaster, and Mathilde endured humiliation for six years. She accompanied her husband first to Saint Petersburg, where she was befriended by Czar Nicholas
I, then the couple moved to Paris, occupying a mansion on rue Saint-Dominique where
Mathilde held her first salon, aged twenty-one.

Mathilde was not truly beautiful, yet was endowed with irresistible charm and intelligence, cultivation and wit. At her Friday salon she received the greatest creative minds
of the day—Baudelaire, Nerval, Chopin, Balzac, Stendhal, Vigny, Delacroix, among others. She separated from her dreadful husband in 1846, supported by the czar who obliged
Demidoff to pay her an annual income of 200,000 francs and leave her half of their magnificent jewelry. Henceforth free and able to spend her fortune as she saw fit, she became
the mistress of the handsome comte de Nieuwekerque, moving to a private residence on
rue de Courcelles. Two years later, the rise to power of her cousin Louis-Napoleon thrust
her to the forefront of the Paris social scene. Her salon was always full, as was the fine
house she bought in Saint-Gratien, near Lake d'Enghien. Starting in 1852, the brilliance
of her soirées in her new Parisian mansion (also on rue de Courcelles) began to make the
imperial court in the Tuileries Palace resemble a provincial salon—the poor if very beautiful Empress Eugénie was made to seem like a duenna lumbered with official recep-
tions. The empire's high society preferred to tread the precious carpets on rue de
Courcelles—whose astonishing decoration included exotic conservatory-salons featuring tropical plants as well as furnishings in every style from every land—where it rubbed
elbows with Mathilde's artist friends: the Goncourt brothers, Alexandre Dumas, George
Sand. Her closest friends included Sainte-Beuve (the critic who lived a scandalous life
but who introduced her to classical literature), Théophile Gautier (a penniless poet

Queen Victoria at her open-air desk, with her faithful
Indian servant, Abdul Karim, in 1893.

enamored of Mathilde, who obtained for him a post of librarian and a comfortable income), and finally Gustave Flaubert (also enamored of her, as proven by the numerous letters he wrote to her). It was at Saint-Gratien, during five summer afternoons in 1869, that Flaubert read aloud for the first time the manuscript of his novel *A Sentimental Education.*

The collapse of the Second Empire threatened Mathilde's position at the center of Parisian high society. She took refuge in Belgium, where she received Flaubert, who had come to comfort her and to escape the Prussian occupation of Paris and the rise of the Commune. Princess Mathilde returned incognito to Paris in June 1871. The French republicans spared her—unlike the other Bonapartes—and President Thiers protected

her. Mathilde moved into a new residence on rue de Berri with the things she had managed to salvage, and opened her salon once again. Some friends were gone, but new ones
arrived, such as Guy de Maupassant and scientists Louis Pasteur and Claude Bernard.
She continued to draw and paint, and began to write. In 1874, her companion for the previous five years, painter and enameler Claudius Popelin, wrote to Edmond de Goncourt:
"She has finally gotten down to it, and when she has done a little bit, she is very happy,
admiring herself almost childishly for having produced a piece of a book. When she has
eight or ten pages, I copy them out, because you know what her handwriting is like, and
she is incapable of copying herself."

Indeed, Mathilde finally began the journal she had been wanting to write for so
long. She darkened many pages with her illegible penmanship—patiently copied by others—and this new activity was to occupy her for many years. It probably spurred the visit
she made to her friend Cartier in October 1876: she wanted to see his pens. She intended
to choose one for herself and another for Popelin. She wanted them to go with the writing implements on her desk at Saint-Gratien—a Louis XV desk (described by Edmond de
Goncourt in 1872) with an inkwell formed by a brass bowl held by a silvered eagle, a san-
dalwood paper knife inlaid with mother-of-pearl, large scissors, and a small datebook.
She also hoped that the beautiful new pen would encourage her to write more legibly.
Many of her friends were members of the Société Française de Graphologie (French
Handwriting Society), founded in 1871 by Abbé Jean-Hippolyte Michon, and were enthusiastic about this new science. Indeed, handwriting analysis was one of the favorite pas-
times at Saint-Gratien. Analysis of Mathilde's own indecipherable handwriting
suggested a strange mixture of modesty—indeed, a penchant for secrecy—and disor-
ganized impulsiveness, which she did not like in the least.

Alfred Cartier issued instructions and a salesman soon brought a few items on a
velvet tray. There were traditional dip pens with long shafts of tortoiseshell tipped with
silver, but above all there was a wide selection of slim cylinders of silver or gold, either
plain or patterned (guilloche or trefoil), or set with turquoise. These pens and mechanical pencils (or "propelling pencils") pleased women in particular: only four inches long,
in two parts that unscrewed, they were endowed with a little ring so that they could be

Porte crayons

Date		N°	Nom	Description		Date		N°	
Février	15	1	Riottot	Cachet Jaspe, à bans or gravé	"	71 Aout	17	1	Comptant
"	"	2	"	Cachet jaspe rond guilloché	"	71 Aout	4	2	"
"	"	3	"	Jaspe incrusté très petit or gravé	"				
1868 x^b	5	4	Occasion	Porte-plume et crayon or gravé	"	71 Aout	34	4	Comptant
"	"	"			"	"	"	"	"
"	"	5	Julien Adelbert	Or rouge uni spirale or rouge poli	"	71 Juillet	27	5	Nicole
"	"	6	"	" " " "	"	71 Juin	30	6	Comptant
1869 x^b	20	7	Riottot	Or mal uni	"	71 8bre	19	7	Comptant
"	"	8	Riottot	Cachet Jaspe or poli	"	19 Janvier	18	8	Comptant
"	"	"		guilloché grains d'orge	"	"	"	"	"
"	"	9	Riottot			70 Juillet	6	9	de Formeville
"	"	"	"	Porte-mine or rouge poli		"	"		"
1872 Janvier	25	10	Feroy	1 Porte mine or mal	"	72 x^{bre}	13	10	Comptant
"	"	11	"	1 Porte mine poli	"	72 Mai	18	11	Comptant
"	"	12		1 Porte mine mat	"	75 Mai	31	12	Reporté n° 41
"	"	13		1 Porte mine poli	"	72 Sept	19	13	de Nicolaï
"	"	14		1 Porte mine mat	"	75 Mai	31	14	Reporté n° 42
"	"	15		1 Porte mine poli	"	70 Juillet	17	15	Comptant
"	"	16	Webert	1 porte mine en or	"	72 x^b	10	16	Comptant
1872 x^b	20	18	"	1 porte mine or rouge petit modèle		72 Avril	27	18	Comptant
" 8bre		19	Khan	Or rouge poli		73 Juillet	30	19	Ducasse
		20	"	" "		77 Mai	31	20	Comptant
		21	"	Or rouge poli		78 Février	6	21	Comptant

worn like a watch on the end of a chain or ribbon. Others were designed more for men, such as those in the shape of a cannon.

On that day in 1876, Alfred Cartier must have encouraged the princess to choose an item that he himself preferred. It was not only handsome but clever, because designed for two uses: an amazing calendar-pencil in guilloche silver. He was far from imagining that half a century later this kind of object would become one of the firm's specialties, since he had been vainly showing it to customers for over a year. Mathilde, for that matter, did not want it either, and Cartier never managed to sell it. Perhaps it was too original for clients at the time. Although curious, tolerant, and open to novelty, Mathilde (nicknamed "Our Lady of the Arts") would always remain very conventional in her tastes. The first Impressionist exhibition two years earlier had stirred a good deal of controversy in the press, and her salon friends spoke of it passionately, yet she herself never frequented the Impressionists and always preferred official artists and "history painters" such as Antoine-Auguste Hébert, one of her best friends. Alfred knew Mathilde well. He knew that she liked drawing even more than writing, and he showed her a curiosity: a little pen with a tip that unscrewed and contained a pencil. The princess could not resist it. She chose a model in red guilloche-patterned gold, and a similar one in plain gold for Popelin. It is not known whether she kept this pen-and-pencil until her death in 1904 (as she did certain items that Cartier had sold her, such as a bracelet adorned with the imperial bee, bought in 1862). Shortly before her death, Our Lady of the Arts still reigned over a salon attended by Proust, sitting—as Abel Hermant described her—"in a comfortable, styleless armchair which nevertheless took on the air of a throne when she sat in it . . . Almost eighty years old, she could still bare her shoulders in grand ceremonial décolleté and wear no other jewelry than a string of large, black pearls."

⋘

Hence it is clear—as demonstrated by Franco Cologni and Ettore Mocchetti in their book, *Made by Cartier*—that right from the start Cartier sold items other than jewelry. On opening his first store on rue Montorgueil in 1847, young Louis-François Cartier, who trained with jeweler Adolphe Picard, was encouraged in this eclecticism by his father, Pierre. As an artisan who specialized in the precious decoration of rifle butts and powder flasks,

A page from the **stock ledger** for mechanical pencils between 1860 and 1872. The entries note the date the item entered stock, the name of the craftsman (or workshop) who made it, an accurate description (occasionally with a drawing), the date of its sale, and sometimes the name of the buyer. Cartier Archives.

Pierre Cartier was as talented at combining metals as he was at working leather or carving ivory. Through experience, he knew that an artisan or small business would be better prepared to withstand the vagaries of commerce by avoiding specialization in a single field; Pierre realized that it was absurd to think of the "luxury market" in terms of totally distinct sectors. Furthermore, Louis-François was a beginner who had to prove his worth. Even if his talent was obvious, even if he excelled in designing the neoclassical, Gothic and Renaissance jewelry then in fashion, nothing yet proved that he could build a clientele with those items alone. Louis-François followed his father's advice, and even registered his business as a "maker of jewels, costume jewelry, millinery, and novelties." That is why he sold not only precious jewelry but also fans, cufflinks, buttons (adorned, true enough, with cameos), busts of bronze and porcelain, precious plates and watches, cane handles and, of course, starting in the 1860s, writing accessories. First came pen stands in jasper or platinum then, from 1868 onward, dip pens and mechanical pencils. The very first writing implement that Louis-François offered his customers was a combined pen and pencil of engraved gold—already one of those combination items.

Among the items Cartier offered in those years, one merits special mention: a mechanical pencil with "openwork decoration against a platinum ground." It was Cartier's first platinum writing implement, which Alfred displayed in the shop on boulevard des Italiens in 1875. Louis-François was probably the first jeweler to use this non-corroding precious metal, supplied almost exclusively from mines in the Ural Mountains. Beginning with small objects such as cufflinks and rings, Cartier's use of platinum would become a well-established tradition, wedded first of all to diamonds on fabulous diadems and graceful aigrettes, then used on watches in the early twentieth century. To this day, platinum remains one of Cartier's great specialties, as will be seen later.

In 1899, Cartier moved from the boulevard to the heart of Parisian luxury and elegance, rue de la Paix off Place Vendôme. The Ritz had just opened on Place Vendôme, where the finest shirtmaker in the world, Charvet, had long reigned. The new Cartier shop, with its magnificent neoclassical façade of black marble, opened at number 13 rue de la Paix, near other famous jewelers as well as the great fashion house, Worth. There was a close relationship between the Cartier and Worth families, for Alfred's eldest son,

Louis, had married Jean-Philippe Worth's daughter, Andrée-Caroline, the previous year. The 24-year-old Louis henceforth worked with his father, and his influence was already decisive. It was he who suggested this move. It was he who would soon take charge of the Paris branch. Highly refined and cultivated, a lover of eighteenth-century French art yet attentive to novelty and open to change, able to attract the most talented designers, Louis would be the soul of Cartier for forty years.

In the "Belle Époque," as the early 1900s were known, Cartier had become one of the most famous jewelers in the world. The cream of international society—from Edward VII of England to opera divas via wealthy businessmen and bankers—blithely strolled through the door of 13 rue de la Paix, where Cartier displayed a dazzling selection of jewelry distinguished by its classic "garland" style and the use of platinum. Louis was not a

great fan of Art Nouveau—called "Modern Style" at the time—and left that style to fellow jeweler René Lalique. Art Nouveau's often overly mannered decoration laden with foliate tendrils and neo-Gothic curves led Paul Morand to dub it the "noodle" style. Cartier in those days favored a Louis XVI classicism, handled with incomparable virtuosity. However, faithful to his great-grandfather's guiding principle, Louis retained—and would later expand—his line of accessories and everyday items. Nothing prevented a marquess or baron, after having chosen splendid rose-cut diamonds to be set in a dog-collar necklace, laurel-leaf diadem or lily-spray brooch, to add the small bonus of a wrist watch, silver picture frame, cigarette-holder, lorgnette or pen. Nothing prevented King Edward VII, on December 20, 1902, from buying a magnifying glass in gold and white enamel, with a plain handle of opaque white enamel wreathed in blue ribbon. The magnificence of these everyday objects was underscored by the elegant cases in which they were also presented, and also matched the plush atmosphere of a shop that glittered with fabulous gems. Some were designed by Cartier, while others were commissioned from specialized artisans, which was the case with the very precious writing tools consisting of traditional dip pens (always featuring gold nibs) and mechanical pencils. In Paris, up to the 1930s, many of these were made in Henri Lavabre's jewelry workshop, where some twenty highly skilled artisans worked on Cartier items.

At a time when people wrote a great deal, when ink pens and mechanical pencils were highly personal everyday items, many celebrities were seduced by these wonders, including divas Nellie Melba and Lina Cavalieri, aviator Alberto Santos-Dumont, society king Boniface de Castellane, and banker J.P. Morgan. People wrote a great deal, in fact, because pens and pencils were the sole means of long-distance communication. People sent hand-written invitations, left annotated calling cards to indicate they had passed by, and wrote countless letters to friends and lovers (even those in a nearby neighborhood) for a trifle—to say hello, to suggest a recipe, to ask news of one's health. In short, to do everything we now do by telephone. In 1900, however, the telephone was still a machine that worked much more efficiently in a Jules Verne novel than in reality. Invented in the United States in 1876, it arrived in France the following year, but twenty years later was still a wooden box bolted to the wall, supplied with an earpiece and a mouthpiece that

RIGHT: **Place Vendôme**, Paris, circa 1900, with rue de la Paix in the background.

dangled from hooks, and a large button that you had to push to alert the switchboard operator. There was no telephone book because there were no telephone numbers. In a droll passage, Comtesse Jean de Pange recounted the difficulty of placing a call in those days: "'Halloo, halloo! Can you hear me, Miss? Do you hear? . . . Answer me, then, Miss! . . . Halloo, halloo! . . . Any insolence, Miss, and I'll lodge a complaint! Halloo, get me the marquise de Luppé, 39 rue Barbet-de-Jouy. Halloo! Yes, Luppé with two Ps, that's right. No, no, Miss, I said 39, not 49 . . .' And after half an hour of exasperation and palaver, you find yourself connected to the Opera or the Morgue! . . . The strangest thing was that the telephone in no way seemed designed for serious business. My father's secretary, who worked in the political office on the ground floor, never used it. Neither did my father. We continued to harness the carriage to send letters or messages into town."

That is why, on March 28, 1902, the great prima donna Nellie Melba bought from Cartier a sliding gold mechanical pencil decorated with two rows of rose-cut diamonds and a cabochon ruby. It might be supposed that the diamonds formed a ring around the object, and that the ruby was set on the tip of the cap. A cabochon gem placed on that spot soon became the emblematic sign of Cartier pens, an emblem that has endured. As to Melba, she was then at the height of her fame. It is hard to imagine today the adulation given to opera singers back then; they unleashed passions and tyrannized their entourages until they were dethroned in the 1920s by stars from Hollywood. Melba was one of those. Born Helen Mitchell in Melbourne, Australia, in 1861, she married young, divorced immediately and headed for London and fame in 1886, taking only a voice that would go down in history for its soft, silvery, crystalline timbre, enhanced by incomparable phrasing, accuracy, agility and evenness. Although some people complained of her coldness, Melba become the most famous soprano of her generation. After several advanced vocal lessons and a difficult start, her diva's career began in 1890 with the role of Marguerite in *Faust*, which she sang in Paris and London. By 1902 she had become the grand, unchallenged prima donna of Covent Garden, where she selected the repertoire herself, secured the best roles (she played Mimi in *La Bohème* for over ten years), and fended off all singers who might resemble her in any way. She became very rich, had many romantic affairs—the most scandalous being with French duke Louis-Philippe,

RIGHT: **Dip pen** (1907) with gold nib and cylindrical barrel of blond tortoiseshell. The lower section is opaline enamel on gold with a wavy guilloche pattern, ringed by two rows of white enamel beads. Art de Cartier Collection.

son of the comte de Paris—and dazzled people with her dresses and jewelry, which she often wore on stage. Cartier was her official jeweler. A famous anecdote recounts how poor Victor Dautremont, a young assistant of Louis Cartier's brother, Pierre (who was running the London branch), had to take her jewels to her dressing room in Covent Garden and warm them before she put them on, to avoid the contact of cold on her skin.

Cartier designed wonderful things for Melba, including a splendid opal pendant in the shape of a heart. In London, meanwhile, the great chef Auguste Escoffier created in her honor a delicious dessert he called "pêche Melba": a peach was peeled, poached in vanilla syrup, allowed to cool, set on a thick layer of vanilla ice-cream, and finally topped with raspberry sauce. One day the prima donna discovered this pure delight on her plate at the Savoy Hotel, and she scrupulously wrote down the recipe in one of her five note-books, bound in black or gold leather, bought from Cartier between 1904 and 1906. And she probably used one of the many mechanical pencils that she acquired from her favorite jeweler between 1902 and 1925. Cartier also supplied her, in April 1905, with a tortoiseshell pen with a lower section of silver gilt and blue enamel, decorated with gold bay leaves; and in 1908, a square eraser with two ends, the middle being enameled in tiny blue-gray and white stripes. Nellie seems to have written many love letters, and apparently often had second thoughts about the wording.

One of Melba's rivals, Lina Cavalieri, was much bolder. And much more beautiful. Photographs show a glowing young brunette whose perfect figure and graceful face with enchanting profile led magazines to call her "the most beautiful woman in the world." Cecil Beaton, in his memoirs, would recall the sorrowful perfection of her Italian face, dominated by large, dark, friendly eyes beneath eyebrows raised not in wonder, but inner sorrow; he said her moving yet sensual mouth was worthy of a painting by Murillo. So beautiful was Cavalieri that, born poor in Rome, she would successfully launch a line of cosmetics and marry first a Russian prince and later an American billionaire. She also performed in all the opera houses in the world, despite debatable talent. She was irresistible in the role of Thaïs, and triumphed in Fedora, the title role of an opera by Giordano, which she premiered in Paris—alongside Caruso—wearing a Cartier diadem. She created a scandal in 1906 and became lastingly famous by passionately kissing her

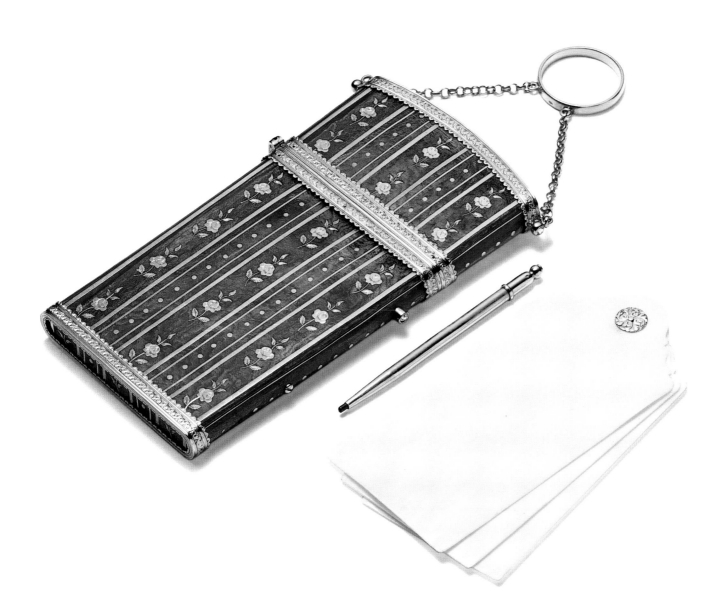

partner Caruso on the mouth during the New York premier of *Fedora*. The next day, the event made the front page of all the New York dailies, which dubbed her "the kissing prima donna." Henceforth she would always travel with bodyguards. In 1907 she premiered *Thaïs* in Paris on June 17th, and several days later went to Cartier to buy a dip pen of blond tortoiseshell and pale green enamel, decorated with two fillets of white enamel. Cavalieri thoroughly enjoyed writing and wrote well, in fact. She retired in the 1930s to a palazzo in Florence, where she wrote a fine book of memoirs, *Le Mie verità* (My Truths), only to die tragically during an air raid on February 7, 1944.

Another emblematic figure of the Belle Époque was Brazilian aviator Alberto Santos-Dumont, a friend of Louis Cartier's. He too wrote a volume of memoirs (*My Airships: The Story of My Life*) and also came to a tragic end. The young Alberto was only eighteen when, in 1892, he inherited a fabulous fortune from his father, Henrique Dumont, the Brazilian "coffee king" and son of a French immigrant. Alberto immediately left the plantation in Brazil and moved to Paris. The first heavier-than-air craft in history, invented by Clément Ader, had only flown two years earlier, and Alberto became fascinated with the idea of flying. He made his first balloon flight on March 23, 1898, between Vaugirard and the grounds of the Château de la Ferrière, owned by Alphonse de Rothschild. This flight whetted Santos-Dumont's appetite, and he began to invest his fortune in dirigible balloons. He designed his own craft, christening each new, improved model with the name *Santos-Dumont*. In 1900, he decided to take up the challenge set by manufacturer Henry Deutsch de la Meurthe, who was offering a prize of 100,000 francs to the first daredevil who could take off in an airship from the Aéro-Club de France in Saint-Cloud, fly to the Eiffel Tower, circumnavigate it, and land again at Saint-Cloud. After several unsuccessful attempts, Santos-Dumont pulled off the exploit on October 19, 1901, aboard the *Santos-Dumont VI*. He became not only famous but extremely popular, having donated half the prize money to the poor of Paris. As inspired as he was whimsical, Santos-Dumont's exploits kept him on the front pages: on June 14, 1903, he landed *Santos-Dumont IX* in the middle of the racetrack at Longchamps, and ten days later flew the same airship to his apartment on the Champs-Elysées, taking off once again on July 14th to fly over the Bastille Day parade at Longchamps, firing twenty-one

PRECEDING PAGES: The famous diva **Nellie Melba** (1861–1931) bought Cartier writing accessories, including five notebooks. The one shown here, similar to one she owned, was made by Cartier in 1910 from tortoiseshell, gold, and diamonds. Art de Cartier Collection.

shots from his revolver as a salute to the French president! These droll eccentricities did not stop with flying—the press published a photo of Santos-Dumont having lunch at home perched on a chair two meters high, seated at a table of the same height, attended by a servant on a stepladder.

Santos-Dumont was already a friend and customer of Louis Cartier when, in 1901, King Leopold of Belgium gave him a pocket watch designed by the jeweler. But this kind of watch was impractical for a pilot constantly at the helm of his airship. Cartier was consulted, and offered to make a wristwatch, although not one mounted on a richly decorated bracelet, like those he had been offering female customers for several years. No, this would be a very sober gold watch held by a simple leather strap, limited to its natural

In 1904, Cartier designed one of the first modern wristwatches for aviator **Alberto Santos-Dumont** (seen here in 1901, Cartier Archives). Santos-Dumont bought a gold mechanical pencil from the jeweler in 1909.

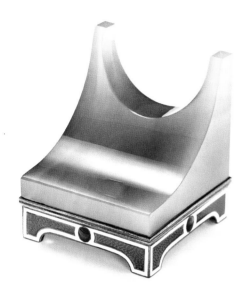

Louis Cartier's friend **Comte Boniface de Castellane**

(1867–1932) was one of the most extravagant celebrities

of the Belle Époque. ABOVE: A gray agate **pen holder**

on an enamel base (1908). FOLLOWING PAGE: At a

time when books were sold with uncut pages, a **paper

knife** was an indispensable object, and remained so

until the 1950s. This nephrite paper knife (1913) boasted

a gold handle with Ionic motif and four cabochon

sapphires, and was one of three paper knives

bought from Cartier by Aga Khan III in the 1910s.

Art de Cartier Collection.

function. That is how Cartier produced, in 1904, one of the first modern wristwatches—which the famous Brazilian immediately adopted. Starting in 1906, Santos-Dumont abandoned dirigibles and began designing airplanes, accomplishing several exploits: that same year he was the first person officially to fly a plane more than 100 meters; on September 16, 1909, he broke the take-off record, managing to get airborne in only 70 meters thanks to his graceful *Demoiselle* motored by a 30-horsepower Darracq engine. It might be supposed that he was wearing, that day, not only the Cartier wristwatch but also a very fine implement acquired from his friend Louis on rue de la Paix just a dozen days earlier—a mechanical pencil in unburnished gold set with a cabochon sapphire. Santos-Dumont abandoned the skies in subsequent years, depressed both by the first signs of arteriosclerosis and by the intuition that his beloved airplanes would soon become engines of death. Increasingly ill and depressed, he took his own life in 1932.

Another exceptional, if less tragic, Belle Époque character was the famous society figure Boniface de Castellane, known as "Boni." Perhaps no one would have ever heard of this minor, bankrupt nobleman if, one fine day in the spring of 1895, he hadn't married one of the richest women in the world—Anna Gould, daughter of an American railroad magnate. Anna may have been one of the world's richest women, but she was also alleged to be one of the least attractive. A guest at the wedding, the duchesse de Gramont, noted that she was "small and thin, her face completely occupied by a large nose and two enormous dark eyes," and that "long black hairs dotted her back." Much later, Boni himself would sum up the situation with his usual caustic humor: "The first time I saw Anna, I thought she wasn't bad at all—given the dowry." The dowry, indeed, was colossal (fifteen million dollars), and the splendor with which the couple set up in Paris symbolized the magnificent, showy extravagance of certain Belle Époque nabobs. This was certainly noted by Louis Cartier, who became Boni's close friend, enjoying his humor and sharing his taste in art (especially eighteenth-century art). Indeed, bankrupt once again after his divorce in 1906, Boni would manage to live comfortably by becoming an art dealer and interior decorator. The pink marble palace that he had built on avenue du Bois had become just a memory—for Boni, at least—as had the extravagantly lavish parties he gave there, including one that required six hundred valets in red livery for the service, two

hundred musicians for the entertainment, and thousands of Chinese lanterns for the lighting. Also a memory was the yacht with its crew of one hundred, and his two châteaux (including one, at Grignan, that had belonged to Madame de Sévigné). All that was left to Boni were his happy memories, such as the time he received a bullet in the thigh during a duel with a reporter from *Le Figaro* who had accused him, in 1901, of squandering his wife's fortune. Yet perhaps Boni kept something more than memories, namely a blond tortoiseshell pen decorated in fine green enamel stripes and gold bands, set with two rings of white enamel beads, purchased from his friend Cartier in October 1905.

Flighty socialites, eccentric millionaires, and capricious prima donnas were not the only people who wanted to write with handsome pens during the Belle Époque. They were joined by the captains of industry and finance, sometimes rather austere men whose signatures were nevertheless worth millions of dollars. And then there were crowned heads and aristocrats who were sufficiently sophisticated and cultured to want to refine their acts of penmanship. Bankers and princes would often cross paths at places like Cartier, as the firm's archives show. One such encounter might be plausibly reconstructed from the wonderful coincidence of an identical purchase by two famous customers on the same day: on Saturday, June 16, 1906, a tall and solidly built young man aged roughly thirty, with swarthy skin and wearing thick glasses, entered the shop on rue de la Paix. The salesmen immediately recognized Aga Khan III. Since 1902, the date of his first purchase—a heart-shaped corsage ornament made of diamonds—this fabulously rich prince of Persian ancestry had become a regular client (as hereditary imam of the Isma'ili Shi'ite Muslims, the Aga Khan claimed direct descent from the prophet Mohammed and the Fatimid caliphs of Egypt). The previous year, he had bought six magnificent Louis XIV brooches. Everyone knew that these jewels would adorn the bodies of the beautiful young women charmed by the prince during his many European trips. Such women helped him forget his obese wife—and cousin—Shahzadi, who remained in India and whom he hardly ever saw. As soon as the salesmen saw the Aga Khan, however, they were flustered and apologetic: "Mr. Cartier is busy with another client, so if His Highness wouldn't mind taking a seat . . ." The young prince realized that if he were being asked to wait, then the other client must be very important indeed. His eyes

Portrait of **Aga Khan III** (1877–1957), circa 1911, in a Cartier frame. Art de Cartier Collection. Portrait of **John Pierpont Morgan** (1837–1913) in a Cartier frame (circa 1910). Cartier Archives.

scanned the shop for Louis Cartier and spotted him in the accessory department with a heavy old man whose drooping mustache and enormous red nose made his face famous—it appeared regularly in the papers and was the delight of cartoonists. So the prince had little difficulty in recognizing the richest man in the world, American banker John Pierpont Morgan.

Owner of 5,000 miles of railroad, the main shareholder or owner of the largest electric, shipping, and steel firms in the United States (having bought the U.S. Steel Company in 1901 for a billion dollars), J.P. Morgan was famous for his legendary flair, his relentless determination, and his sometimes ferocious authority. And he was also the greatest art collector of his day. Starting in 1890, he began buying all the European art he could lay his hands on, from antique Greek to eighteenth century—thousands of paintings, bronzes, tapestries, furniture, porcelain, rare books, manuscripts, and so on. Among them were many sublime works of art, including Rembrandts and Dürers, marble statues from the Florentine school, and autograph manuscripts by Dickens and Balzac. This eclecticism might seem surprising at first sight, but Morgan was not collecting for himself or to satisfy his own tastes so much as for the American nation, to whom he intended to bequeath this treasure. Following his wishes, it would be primarily divided between the Metropolitan Museum of Modern Art, the Pierpont Morgan Library (both in New York), and the Wadsworth Athenaeum (in Hartford, Connecticut, his home town).

Meanwhile the young prince, who had just turned twenty-nine, liked the idea of meeting this most powerful symbol of American capitalism. He caught hold of a salesman and asked him to take his calling card to Mr. Morgan. Shortly afterward, Louis Cartier came forward and made the introductions. After a few pleasantries, Morgan invited the Aga Khan to sit with them. Salesmen were showing the old magnate calling-card cases. He had already chosen one for himself, a large case in finely reeded gold with a ruby clasp. Morgan wanted another one, to present to a lady. Having heard of the prince's savoir-faire in such matters, he asked the Aga Khan for advice. The latter unhesitatingly recommended a similar model also tipped with a ruby, but of smaller dimensions. Morgan concurred and set it aside. The Aga Khan then turned to Louis Cartier and

60

asked if he had another case just as perfect, which he would like to buy himself. The jeweler reassured the prince that two copies of the model existed. And that is how, in the same place on the same day, a magnificent oriental prince and an American financial magnate bought the same object.

The Aga Khan (one of whose sons, Ali Aga Khan, would marry first Joan Guiness and then Rita Hayworth) did not buy any writing implements from Cartier. He did, however, acquire three wonderful paper knives in the 1910s: one was white jade with an ivory handle, the other was in silver gilt (also with ivory handle), and the third in nephrite with a gold handle decorated in black enamel and set with four cabochon sapphires (this last item has been recovered by Cartier and now features in its "Art de Cartier Collection," to be discussed below). J.P. Morgan, meanwhile, was an enthusiastic collector of autographs, and one of the biggest fans of the precious pens and pencils sold by Cartier in those years. From 1890 until his death in 1913, Morgan was more a collector than a businessman, leaving the management of his empire to associates. He went often to Europe, scouring the antique shops and auction rooms in the company of the experts in his employ. Moored in the Mediterranean was his 300-foot yacht, *Corsair III*, which he would sail to the Nile where his large motorized *cangia*, or riverboat, was waiting. Morgan owned several estates in England, plus private rooms reserved all year round in the Grand Hotel in Rome and the Hotel Bristol in Paris. That is where he became friends with Louis Cartier. The two men met often—sharing a passion for books, among other things—both in Paris and New York, where Cartier was regularly received at the fine Morgan residence on the corner of Madison Avenue and 36th Street. Meanwhile, in 1908 Louis's brother Pierre, who would soon head the New York branch, married Elma Rumsey, the daughter of one of Morgan's main business partners (their daughter, Marion, would marry the son of French writer Paul Claudel). Morgan bought splendid jewelry from Cartier, including the 35-carat drop diamond that now bears his name, plus a "winged tiara," a "sun tiara," a necklace with an engraved, 105-carat emerald and 70-carat sapphire, and a heart-shaped pocket watch in platinum studded with diamonds. Yet the striking thing revealed by the firm's archives is the number of writing implements bought by the banker, who spent a small fortune on them. In October 1906, he bought a blond tortoiseshell pen featuring

Pierre Cartier (1878–1965), director of Cartier New York, pictured in 1910. RIGHT: A **mechanical pencil** (1906) in the form of a feather, with pink enamel guilloche pattern on gold, edged with gray enamel stripes and white beads. The push-rod is a rose-cut diamond. This pencil belonged to Baron Henri de Rothschild. Art de Cartier Collection. FOLLOWING PAGES: This **desk set** (1908), in enamel and gold with a wavy guilloche pattern, is typical of the classical style promoted by Cartier in the early twentieth century. The base is decorated in Louis XIV stripes, while the small clock features a diamond-studded motif on top. Art de Cartier Collection.

an enameled silver-gilt lower section, with matching stand; in July 1908, he purchased a large model, gold and green-enamel striped *stylographe* (a term which had just appeared in the ledgers to refer to a pen with its own reservoir of ink, i.e., a fountain pen); in July 1909, he bought two large fountain pens, one enhanced with black and white enamel stripes with white beads, the other in green-striped enamel with white beading; three days later, Morgan bought yet another pen, smaller this time, in gold and white-striped enamel; in October 1910, he was at Cartier's once again to buy a conical pencil in gold and blue-gray enamel, decorated with blue enamel beading and pink flowerets, as well as two mechanical pencils, one in purple enamel, the other in blue-gray enamel. Taking into account other writing and office items (calling-card cases, a nephrite paper knife decorated with sapphires, a magnifying glass, and sapphire seals), the richest man in the world prior to the outbreak of the Great War spent over 5,000 francs on such implements over a four-year period at Cartier (equivalent to approximately $20,000 today).

Louis Cartier would have other magnificent writing tools created for his clients. Some were lavish, others just exquisitely graceful—such as a 1906 mechanical pencil in the shape of a feather (a reminder of the good old quills) in pink enamel on gold, with a rose-cut diamond to advance the lead. It was bought by Baron Henri de Rothschild. Then there were all the little short-handled gold-and-enamel pens equipped with a cap like modern pens so that ladies could drop one in a handbag. Again, starting around 1910, there were the amazing miniature mechanical pencils, nicknamed "Tom Thumb," which would continue to delight clients (including Nellie Melba and the Maharajah of Kapurthala) into the 1930s. There were also clever telescopic pencils in gold, studded with brilliants and endowed with an onyx seal at the end, that collapsed to half their size. The king of Spain, Alphonso XIII, bought a similar model in 1929. Jade and tortoiseshell (blond or brown) were always used abundantly for dip pens. None of these objects in any way reflects the artistic trends of the moment. Cartier's dip pens and fountain pens of the period bore no trace of Art Nouveau decoration, for example, much less of the Japanese fad that began in the 1880s or the Fauvist movement that was launched in 1905. Louis Cartier's taste always tended toward the classic and sober, which sometimes resulted in a style that prefigured

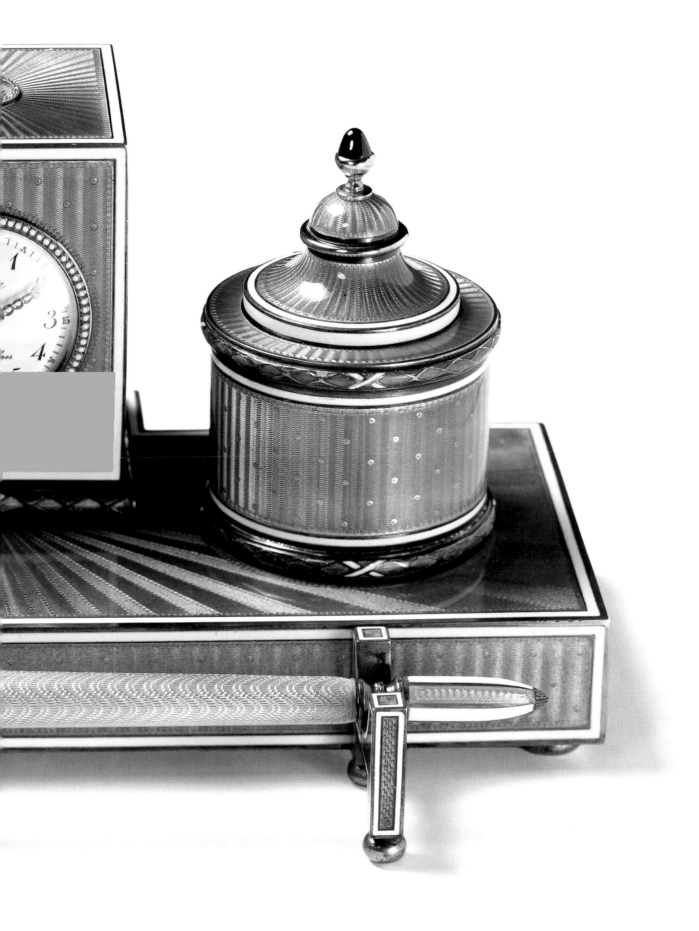

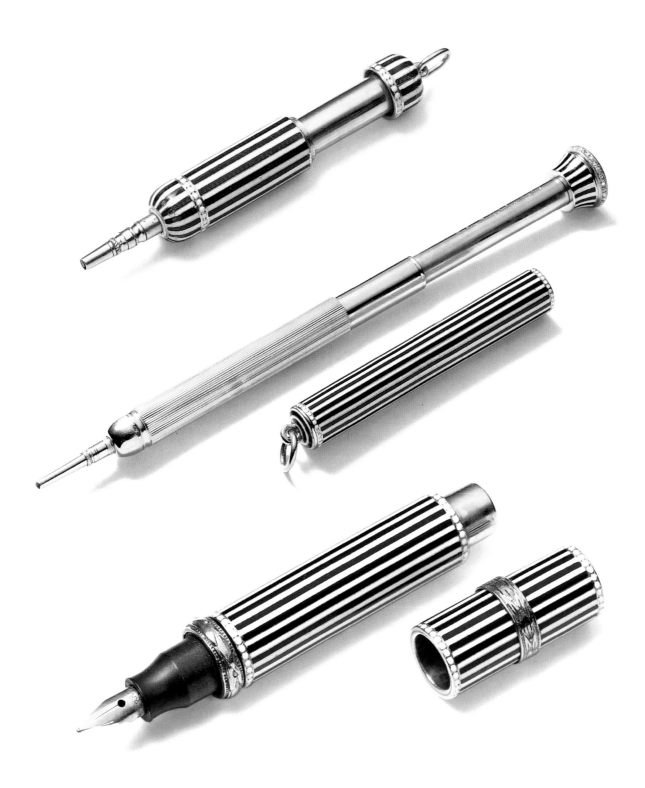

the simple geometry of Art Deco ten or twenty years before that movement emerged. Thus in 1913 Cartier produced an extraordinarily pure ivory dip pen with black enamel bands and onyx tip. Only the use of enamel—also employed for watches and other accessories—reflects the influence of a contemporary, though one marginal to the history of art, namely that of Russian jeweler Fabergé, the great specialist in enameled objects. Louis Cartier admired Fabergé and considered him to be his only worthy rival.

In fact, in those days Cartier felt that writing implements should reflect their times largely in terms of technology rather than aesthetics, which meant a profound understanding of changes in lifestyle. At a time when railroads were expanding, when automobiles were becoming common, and air travel was beginning to revolutionize conventional notions of distance and travel, the standard items of daily life had to be both small and autonomous. Writing implements, for instance, were henceforth carried on the body and had to function without the need for other accessories. That meant they had to be small, have a cap, and above all contain a built-in reservoir for ink, which transformed the traditional dip pen into a fountain pen. Around 1900, the pen manufacturer De La Rue launched an advertising campaign around its Onoto pen, featuring a couple in travel dress writing postcards, standing in front of a steam locomotive, while a slogan in large letters advises: "Never travel without your Onoto fountain pen."

"Endless-writing pens" with "wells," in fact, had existed since the seventeenth century, while pens with built-in reservoirs were developed in the nineteenth. None of those instruments, however, although seeking to fulfill a real need, were truly satisfactory. The methods for getting ink to the nib, in particular, outdid one another in triggering catastrophic effects. The simplest system involved shaking the pen—which usually produced big blotches. More sophisticated methods employed various patented valves, stop-clocks, plungers, baffles, fibrous retarders and rotating rings by the hundreds, none of which produced an even flow of ink. In the early 1880s, a New York insurance salesman named Lewis Edison Waterman nevertheless bought one of these items; Waterman traveled a good deal to sell new policies which had to be signed by the clients, and he felt that his dip pen and "travel" inkwell were inconvenient and cumbersome. Just after making his purchase, Waterman went to a construction site to pay a visit to a major client—a builder—

LEFT, TOP TO BOTTOM: The gold "Tom Thumb" telescopic **mechanical pencil** (1912) with blue and white striped enamel design, plus two rows of white enamel beads. It measures 2.85 cm when closed (5.25 cm when open). Art de Cartier Collection. Telescopic **mechanical pencil** (1912) in fluted yellow gold with black and white striped enamel knob ringed with rose-cut brilliants set in platinum. Traditional **dip pen** (circa 1910) in yellow gold with black and white striped enamel design, ringed with white enamel beads. This one belonged to the duchess of Marlborough. Art de Cartier Collection. FOLLOWING PAGES: The same objects. The "Tom Thumb" pencil is closed.

and get a signature on a policy. He held out the precious document and the brand new pen. The client shook the pen but no ink arrived. He shook again, spattering the contract with ink, but couldn't manage to sign. So he shook harder still, and suddenly a black puddle of ink spread across the document. Waterman apologized, promising to return with a new contract and a proper writing implement. The next day, he learned that the client had taken out a policy with a competitor.

Waterman discovered that no "fountain pen" then on the market worked any better. So, as an inspired tinkerer, he set out to attack the tricky problem himself. He soon realized that only a channel that permitted both ink and air to circulate could supply a regular flow. After numerous experiments, he managed to develop a capillary tube from an ebonite cylinder etched with a three-channel feed, for which he applied for a patent on February 12, 1884. This date represents the birth of truly modern pens—all subsequent models would be based on this technique. The extremely efficient and simple system sprang from the brain of an insurance salesman with no degree (and who had formerly been a carpenter and stenography teacher). Waterman's pen worked so well that all his friends asked him to make them one—that is how he wound up becoming a pen manufacturer. "Waterman's Ideal Fountain Pen" was guaranteed for five years. Two hundred were made the first year, five hundred the second. The third year, an advertising man came to his aid, and thousands of orders began flowing in. Waterman had to build two factories and the Waterman Pen Company enjoyed considerable success. Other pen inventors and manufacturers—George Parker, Walter Shaeffer, Roy Conklin—subsequently made major improvements to the system of filling the reservoir, such as Conklin's "crescent filler," a metal crescent affixed to the body of the pen to apply pressure to the rubbery reservoir.

Fountain pens made their appearance at Cartier in 1908. Like traditional dip pens, they all had solid gold nibs. The ledgers of the day do not mention the ink-filling system(s) employed—they probably had to be filled with an eyedropper. But the ledgers describe the "dressing," which was sometimes classic and sober, like the plain polished or guilloche-patterned gold preferred by the duchess of Marlborough and by Jacques Cartier, the third brother, who took over the London branch of the jewelry firm in 1906.

RIGHT: Two examples of the striped pattern from different periods. Top: gold **mechanical pencil** (1908) with white and gold striped enamel design, ringed by two rows of white enamel beads, tipped with polished yellow gold. The lower section has a band of yellow gold engraved with a foliage motif. The cap, also ringed with a foliate band, has two rows of white enamel beads. Bottom: a 1934 **"pen with reservoir"**—that is to say, fountain pen—in yellow gold, decorated with black enamel fillets. The tip is polished yellow gold and the pen is endowed with a pressure filling system. The cap is decorated with the same black enamel lines. Art de Cartier Collection.

Yet the dressing might often be more elaborate, like the pens chosen by the wife of American magnate and art patron Cornelius Vanderbilt (enameled gold ringed with sapphires), Baron James de Rothschild (pink enamel) and Prince Radziwill (black and white striped enamel). By 1911, Louis Cartier was also offering his clients pens manufactured by Waterman, decorated according to his own instructions in plain or guilloched white gold, ringed with rose-cut diamonds, and enhanced by a cabochon sapphire. By the time World War I had ended, the House of Cartier was selling the finest models by the best manufacturers, including Waterman, Conklin, and Montblanc. Later it would become, in turn, a great penmaker in its own right.

Jacques Cartier (1884–1942), director of Cartier London from 1906 onward. Cartier Archives.

CHAPTER III

The Roaring Twenties
and Oriental Elegance

PRECEDING PAGE: Silver **mechanical pencil** with built-in watch and lighter (left), and both halves of a combination **pen** and **pencil with watch** (right, see p. 91). ABOVE: Three gold **mechanical pencils** with calendar, 1927. Cartier Archives. RIGHT, TOP TO BOTTOM: Telescopic **fountain pen** (circa 1926) of polished and fluted gold, with English calendar on the cap. Gold **telescopic pencil** with calendar (1927). Blue enamel letters and numerals except for a red D for *Dimanche* (Sunday). Gold **telescopic pencil** with calendar (1927). The month is displayed in a little window. Art de Cartier Collection.

T

he horror of World War I extinguished the last illusory glimmers of the Belle Époque. And for some people, the era of unbridled pleasure died along with it, among the mourning, the ruins, the revolutions. That was true of many of Europe's ruling families—the Romanovs, the Hohenzollerns, the Hapsburgs—and of the aristocracies they headed, who were the buyers of Cartier's most magnificent items. Louis reacted and built a new clientele by increasing the sale of more affordable jewelry and everyday objects. Writing implements multiplied, as beautiful as ever, in particular the fountain pens which were gradually replacing traditional dip pens.

The war naturally sparked a major need to write. Never had people corresponded so much, what with worried families and soldiers who, faced with death, felt an urge to confide. In France, the military and civilian postal services delivered four million letters per day at the start of the war, rising to over ten million per day by 1918! And for a soldier in the field, nothing was better for writing than one of the new fountain pens with built-in ink reservoir and cap, since it could be easily carried and didn't require the simultaneous use of a cumbersome inkwell. All the soldiers in the American contingent had one, and French *poilus* (doughboys) thus discovered an object that most of their fellow citizens had not yet seen. The Parker company even developed a "trench pen" for American soldiers, endowed with a system for carrying ink safely (the first ink cartridges would only hit the market twenty years later)—ink was sold in tiny water-soluble pellets that could be placed directly in the reservoir. Soon Waterman was imitating Parker, and advertised its "Ideal Pen" as being the one most valued on the front.

It was therefore just after the war that a pacified, Americanized Europe became familiar with a new tool that had long been used in the United States. In 1919, Cartier produced a polished gold fountain pen with a perpetual calendar enameled on the barrel, in either French or English. It featured a "pneumatic" filling system that was more reliable than the traditional eyedropper and was less ugly than the various lever systems— as proposed by Conklin, Shaeffer, and Waterman—which ruined the fluid lines of the body of the pen. Removing the cap at the end of the Cartier pen revealed a small rubber ball that was pressed to force air from the empty chamber; then the nib was dipped in the inkwell and the pressure was released.

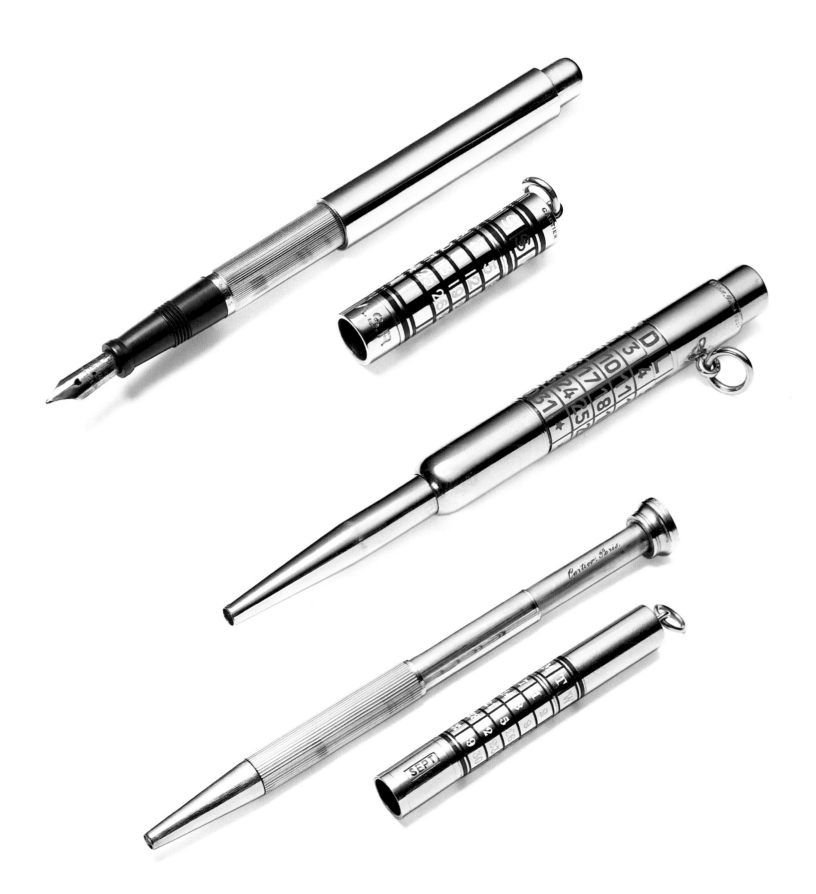

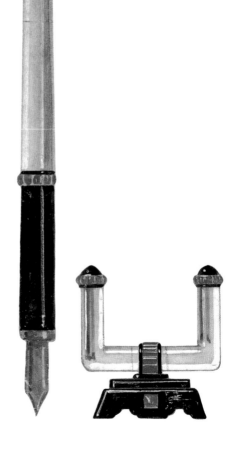

In Europe, these initial improvements were not enough to win over fans of traditional pens. Not only did dip pens remain much less expensive than fountain pens, but French schoolchildren continued to use them into the 1960s, when the spread of plastic led to very cheap fountain and ballpoint pens. Price was not the only reason for reservations, however. It was almost as though the long shape which dip pens had inherited from the old goose quills, along with regular recourse to the inkwell, constituted a more natural form, gesture, and rhythm—more conducive to concentration—that became unconsciously associated with the act of writing. Many writers, even affluent ones, never abandoned their dip pens. Marcel Proust, for example, who suffered from chronic asthma and therefore wrote in bed in the period just before his death, utilized such instruments to the end, however impractical: "The amazing thing was the speed with which he could write in that position, which only he would find comfortable," wrote Proust's faithful housekeeper, Céleste Albaret in her wonderful *Monsieur Proust.* "You had to see the pen fly and string out his tiny, joined letters. The only pens he used were Sergeant-Majors . . . I never saw him use a fountain pen, even though such pens were becoming common at the time. I would buy boxes and boxes of replacement nibs. As to the nib-holder, there were always a good fifteen or so within reach since, if he happened to drop the one he was using, it could not be picked up for fear of dust, except when he wasn't there. They were little iron shafts to hold a nib, the simplest schoolboy model."

In order to satisfy hard-core fans of traditional pens—and also because such items offered greater decorative freedom than fountain pens of the day—Cartier continued to design new dip pens after the war. They were pure marvels, such as the 1925 model with a barrel of gray and amber agate decorated with four bands of coral, its lower section being of yellow gold with little black enamel squares. And then there was the one he sold in 1926 to Harold McCormick, heir to the famous farm machine company—a pen featuring a round barrel of ebonite and ivory with gold trim, adorned at the end with a ring of ivory and a cabochon coral on gold. The pen was probably a present for McCormick's wife, the singer Ganna Walska. Three years later, Walska herself would go to Cartier and select another model, notable for the jeweler's brilliant play of colors and materials (in this case a combination of blond and brown tortoiseshell). During this same period,

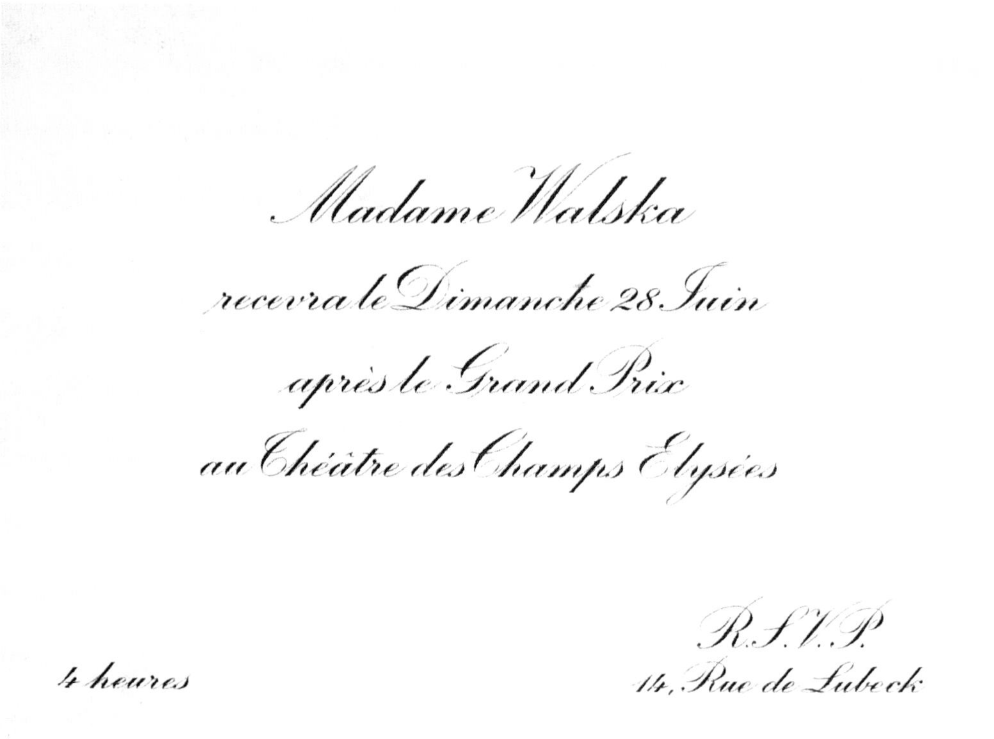

Madame Walska

recevra le Dimanche 28 Juin

après le Grand Prix

au Théâtre des Champs Elysées

4 heures

R.S.V.P.
14, Rue de Lubeck

Cartier designed a Chinese-style pen with black lacquer body, decorated with geometric red and black enameling highlighted by a row of rose-cut diamonds set in platinum. It was accompanied by an amazing stand in yellow gold and enamel, decorated with four diamonds, two coral cylinders, and two cabochon onyxes.

These designs with their pure shapes and lines, whose sophistication resided basically in a bold contrast of colors and the use of noble or precious materials, suddenly made Cartier seem perfectly in step with his times. That was because these pens, like all the other writing tools Cartier designed in those days—inkwells, paper weights, paper knives, datebook holders—clearly reflected the Art Deco style of the 1920s. Right when it first emerged around 1906, Art Deco resolutely opposed Art Nouveau's outmoded mannerism (despite the "new" in Nouveau). Architecture was the first sphere in which this modernist reaction, enamored of machines, functionality, and pure lines, fully

Design for a **retractable mechanical pencil** with chain (circa 1925), in silver, lapis lazuli, and turquoise. Cartier Archives. LEFT: Miniature **telescopic pencil** (1929) with a gold barrel and a cap of black enamel on yellow gold. The square platinum knob is set with emeralds and diamonds, while the cap is topped by a semi-spherical ribbed emerald on a base of diamonds, set off with four cabochon emeralds. The interlinked suspension rings are of platinum, the larger one rimmed with rose-cut diamonds. Here the pencil is placed on a small **gold envelope** made by Cartier. Art de Cartier Collection.

expressed itself. It was prefigured by Adolf Loos in Austria, Auguste Perret in France (who built the first private house in concrete) and the Chicago School in the United States. Then the trend spread to the visual arts via Fauvism, Futurism and Cubism, all of which contributed to the development of Art Deco. Its rise was halted by the Great War, but it returned in force in the 1920s, becoming part of everyday life thanks to designers influenced by Walter Gropius and the Bauhaus, by French architect Robert Mallet-Stevens, by furniture makers such as Jacques-Émile Ruhlmann, by silversmiths such as Jean Puiforcat, and by bookbinders such as Pierre Legrain. The Art Deco movement finally prevailed in Paris at the 1925 Exposition Internationale des Arts Décoratifs et Industriels Modernes. The show's rules stipulated that only works "of new and truly original inspiration" would be admitted, and the twenty exhibiting countries outdid one another in modernity and avant-gardism. The "Pavilion of the New Spirit" was designed by Le Corbusier and decorated with paintings by Juan Gris and Fernand Léger, while an "ideal French Embassy" had twenty-five rooms all decorated by different designers, including Mallet-Stevens and Robert Delaunay. One of the highlights of the show was Konstantin Melnikov's Soviet pavilion, which included a "workers' club" designed by the great Russian avant-garde artist Alexander Rodchenko. The more traditional "Pavilion of Elegance," meanwhile, hosted the great fashion designers of the day—Callot, Worth, Lanvin. That is where Louis Cartier decided to show his designs, rather than in the jewelers' pavilion, probably to underscore the firm's founding spirit, which deplored the division between various types of finery. Fascinated members of the public could thus discover Cartier's jewelry—diadems, earrings, head-bands, and so on. The Art Deco trend was reflected in the more linear cut of the gems, notably baguette cut (which Louis Cartier had long liked), square cut, and emerald cut. Many items were also notable for the juxtaposition of contrasting colors and materials, another general feature of Art Deco. This was true of a piece that remains, even today, emblematic of the House of Cartier, namely the "trinity ring" combining white, pink, and yellow gold; it dates from 1923, allegedly designed for—and on an idea by—Jean Cocteau. Above all, these Art Deco designs, including various accessories and writing implements, owed much to the most brilliant designer at Cartier in those years, Charles Jacqueau, hired in 1909.

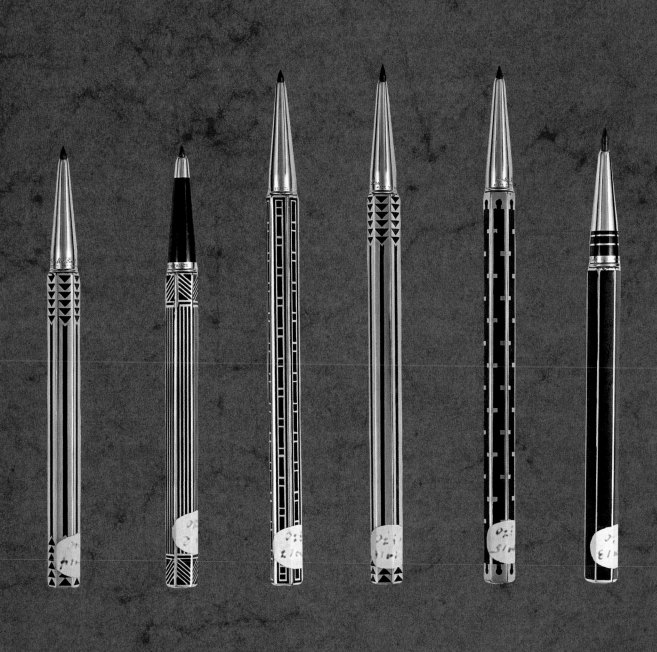

The poet Cocteau was one of the tastemakers of those Roaring Twenties which helped people to forget the great tragedy of war. Cocteau was still young—born in 1889, like the Eiffel Tower, he would remain young until his death in 1963—and became the graceful will-o'-the-wisp of a group of artists who set the tone, and whom Louis Cartier admired and frequented, including Serge Diaghilev, director of the Ballets Russes, composer Igor Stravinsky, opera singer Feodor Shaliapin, novelist Colette, and also the fashion designer Gabrielle Chasnel, or Coco Chanel as she came to be known, who revolutionized feminine dress by inventing the sober, straight, short cut favored by *les garçonnes* (flappers). Those single women, popularized by a best-selling novel of the day, spearheaded a broader movement which brought a radical change to women's status. Their emancipation was one of the powerful ideas of the day, forged during the war when daughters and wives went to work to replace men who were called up. This emancipation called for a new figure—slim, sporty, androgynous, and completely liberated from the frills, lace and ribbons of the doll-like women of yesteryear. The new image was incarnated by the sublime stars of Hollywood—Marlene Dietrich, Louise Brooks, and Greta Garbo. Many female writers also profited from this trend to make a name for themselves. Gone were the days when, around 1900, Princess Bibesco (a great fan of Cartier's pens and jewelry) had to publish her book under a male pseudonym in order to have it taken seriously. When it was learned who was behind the pen-name, a socialite reportedly said to the princess, "You write novels? But that's unbelievable, a woman dressed the way you are!" Colette was already famous by the 1920s and 1930s, and many other women had successful careers in Europe and the United States, including American authors Edith Wharton and Gertrude Stein (who lived in Paris where she was friends with the likes of F. Scott Fitzgerald and Ernest Hemingway) and English writers Agatha Christie and Virginia Woolf.

There was also a woman who established her talent on rue de la Paix alongside Louis Cartier—Jeanne Toussaint, dubbed "the panther." Toussaint was a woman whose intense charm stemmed from a combination of rare natural distinction, great elegance, and a touch of mystery. Louis fell in love with her and she became his companion. Jeanne was not only seductive, however; like her friend Chanel, she displayed outstanding taste

Colette, one of the few French women granted the status of "great writer," became another symbol of female emancipation by refusing to hide what were considered scandalous love affairs at the time. She was photographed by Herbert List in her apartment at the Palais-Royal. PRECEDING PAGES: Art Deco pencils from the 1920s. On the left, a series of telescopic **mechanical pencils** in enameled white gold, with suspension ring and seal (1927). Note variations in Art Deco details (fluting versus geometric frieze) and color combinations (black enamel and onyx versus blue enamel and sapphire). Cartier Archives. On the right are more Art Deco versions of an eight-sided **mechanical pencil** in white gold and black enamel (1928). Cartier Archives.

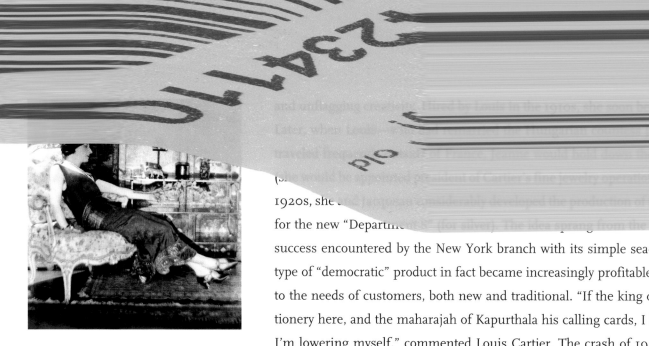

and unflagging creativity. Hired by Louis in the 1910s, she soon became his right hand. Later, when Louis was increasingly absent for things that concerned the business, traveled frequently abroad. The two women would hold down the fort at the rue de la Paix (she would be appointed president of Cartier's fine jewelry operations in 1933). In the late 1920s, she and Jacqueau considerably developed the production of items and accessories for the new "Department S" (for silver). The idea sprang from the amazing commercial success encountered by the New York branch with its simple sea-blue stationery. This type of "democratic" product in fact became increasingly profitable, and responded well to the needs of customers, both new and traditional. "If the king of Spain buys his stationery here, and the maharajah of Kapurthala his calling cards, I hardly feel as though I'm lowering myself," commented Louis Cartier. The crash of 1929 and its disastrous economic and political repercussions would spur Cartier to expand production of these more affordable items, prefiguring a marketing policy that would culminate in the 1970s with the launching of the "Musts de Cartier" line.

In addition to evening bags, clutch bags, vanity cases, travel kits, and smoking accessories, the "Department S" led by Toussaint and Jacqueau produced some of the finest writing and desk implements ever designed. In addition to the dip pens described above, there were extraordinary combination items—which Jacqueau so liked—such as an agate paper knife with a watch set into the silver handle, calendar pens, and ingenious watch pens that combined Cartier's great traditions as a jeweler and a watchmaker. The department even produced a triple combination, a pen that incorporated a watch and a lighter. These accessories were highly sought after by Europe's fashionable elite. In August 1927, Grand Duke Dimitri, cousin of the late czar (as well as being Chanel's lover), bought a mechanical pencil in fluted silver in two detachable parts with a black enamel calendar (in English) in the center, the upper part fitting into a fluted silver sheath. In 1929, Madame Antony de Rothschild acquired a black lacquer and yellow gold datebook cover with built-in watch. During those same years, at Toussaint's instigation once again, Cartier also designed magnificent inkwells and desk sets of jade, agate, and lapis lazuli that combined inkwell, pen stand, vase and clock. One of Toussaint's great friends, the highly attractive Mona Williams (then married to one of the richest men in America, later

Jeanne Toussaint, nicknamed "the panther," was the firm's creative muse for over half a century (above). She is seen here in the 1920s (right), dressed in the oriental style. Cartier Archives. FOLLOWING PAGES: "Department S" designs from the 1920s to 1940s Left: **Mechanical pencil** in yellow gold and black enamel (1928). On the end is a cabochon ruby topped by a platinum stud set with a rose-cut diamond. A **datebook** (1929) in black lacquer and yellow gold with built-in watch and mechanical pencil, which once belonged to Mrs. Antony de Rothschild. Art de Cartier Collection. Right, top to bottom: A triple combination model (circa 1940) incorporating fountain pen, pencil and watch, in fluted silver; two **mechanical pencils** with built-in watch, one in polished yellow gold (1930), the other in fluted silver (1930) with a lighter as well as a pivoting watch cover. Art de Cartier Collection.

Mona Williams, the future Countess Bismarck (here photographed by Cecil Beaton in 1955, in her Paris residence, the Hôtel Lambert), purchased this 19th-century Chinese porcelain **inkwell** with carved wooden base and top, adorned with gold geometric motifs by Cartier in 1927. Art de Cartier Collection.

to become Countess Bismarck) bought two magnificent objects in 1927: a paperweight in the form of a truncated column of nephrite topped by a Chinese "Fo" (Buddhist) dog of ivory, set with a sapphire; and a blood-red Chinese porcelain inkwell decorated by Cartier in yellow gold, with a carved wooden base and top.

It thus appears that an "East wind" was blowing over Cartier in those years—objets d'art included many Art Deco versions of chinoiserie, typified by an abundant use of lacquer, mother-of-pear, jade, coral, and various motifs evoking China. The year 1926 yielded a highly precious Chinese-style mechanical pencil all in coral, crowned with a seated greyhound and adorned with two black enamel bands set with cabochon emeralds and rose-cut diamonds. Japan also invaded rue de la Paix, as seen for example in the fountain pen purchased on Tuesday, November 5, 1929, by a man aged roughly sixty, sporting a large mustache and a pair of thick glasses. Just the previous week, the world had been rocked by the financial earthquake of the Wall Street crash, whose tragic repercussions were already being sensed. The man with thick glasses was not about to panic, however. His fortune was not the kind to go up in smoke, since it was based on his talent as a world-renowned writer. Rudyard Kipling was his name. The Nobel laureate was on a pleasure trip to France, a country he had loved—along with its language—ever since he visited the Universal Exposition at age twelve, in the company of his father. Now he found himself in Cartier's, where he had been told he could find wonderful pens. Kipling was always extremely fond of his writing implements—in his memoirs, *Something of Myself: For My Friends Known and Unknown* (1937), he affectionately described a thin, eight-sided pen made of agate, another of silver in the form of a quill, plus various fountain pens including his favorite, a smooth, black pen bought in Jerusalem. And if he published not a word about the one he bought at Cartier's that day, it is perhaps because he did not write with it very much.

Kipling bought that pen for two special reasons, not the least of which was the delight it afforded the eye. The pen was a Namiki—a legendary name in the world of pen collectors. Founded in 1918 by Ryosuke Namiki and Masao Wada, the Japanese firm of Namiki would later become universally known by the name of Pilot. In addition to everyday objects, in 1920 the company began producing extraordinary pens decorated by the country's best lacquer artists. Every Namiki lacquer pen was thus a unique work of art, created by a true artist. In order to promote them, Cartier—who was still selling fine models by Waterman, Conklin, Montblanc and French penmaker Gold Starry as well as pens of the firm's own design—bought two series, in March and May 1927. As part of a special order, precious bands were added to two of the pens by Cartier artisans. Louis Cartier and Jeanne Toussaint each chose one Namiki for themselves, as did Princess Bibesco. (As of 1930, the Dunhill company obtained sole distributorship for Namiki pens in Europe and the United States.)

When Kipling discovered these costly lacquered treasures, he knew he couldn't resist buying one. Above all, it seemed like an amusing coincidence—on reading newspaper accounts of the dozens of suicides by businessmen ever since the disastrous stock market crash the preceding week, Kipling couldn't stop thinking of the only time in his life when he found himself suddenly bankrupt. That was back in 1892, during his honeymoon to Japan, as it turned out. Already rich and famous at the age of twenty-six, he went to the Yokohama branch of his London bank to withdraw some money. A dismayed employee informed him that the bank had just failed, and that it could no longer honor the tiniest check. The young Kipling thus found himself totally bankrupt, possessing only what he still had in his pocket—just enough to board the first steamer for the United States, his wife's home. He went to his parents-in-law's place in Vermont, where he immediately began producing material for his publishers. Within a matter of weeks, he was a rich man again.

Yet this rather droll episode from his youth was obviously not the only motive for his purchase. Ever since his first visit to the Empire of the Rising Sun, during a trip around the world in 1888, Kipling had become a great lover of Japanese art. The articles written during that voyage for the Allahabad *Pioneer* testify to this enthusiasm, especially for porcelain, cloisonné enamel, and lacquer (after a visit to Kyoto's finest lacquer workshops). Those articles were collected in a book, *From Sea to Sea*, in which Kipling's admiration for Japan overshadowed his political clairvoyance at a time when that country was arming itself and entertaining colonial ambitions: "Japan is a great people. Her masons play with stone, her carpenters with wood, her smiths with iron, and her artists with life,

Chinoiserie abounded at Cartier in the 1920s, when both jewelry and accessories were often decorated with animal motifs, chimeras, or panthers. This nephrite **paperweight** (circa 1927) is topped by an ivory "Fo" dog (a Buddhist symbol) set with a sapphire bead and semi-precious stones. The base is decorated with four cabochon sapphires. It once belonged to Mona, Countess Bismarck. Next to it is a **mechanical pencil** (1926) in carved coral with two bands of emeralds and diamonds, crowned with a seated greyhound. Art de Cartier Collection.

Sell your books at
sellbackyourbooks.com!
Go to sellbackyourBook.com
and get an instant price
quote. We even pay the
shipping - see what your old
books are worth today!

Inspected By: erika_ortiz

00074234110

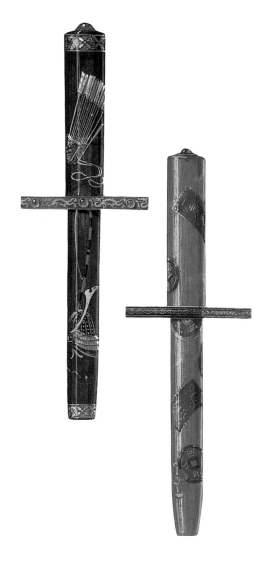

Legendary **Namiki pens** were made of costly lacquer in Japan. Starting in 1927, Cartier sold two series of them, adorning two of the pens with precious bands. The firm's archives contain preparatory designs for these objects (*above*). RIGHT: **Rudyard Kipling**, a great fan of Japanese art (painted here in 1899 by Edward Burne-Jones), acquired a Namiki pen at Cartier Paris in 1929.

death, and all the eye can take in. Mercifully she has been denied the last touch of firmness in her character which would enable her to play with the whole round world. We possess that . . ." Kipling's assessment would soon be contradicted by the facts.

Back in 1929, however, "Japonism" was still enjoying the vogue it had triggered in Europe a half century earlier, and would continue to enjoy for a few years more. In France, the early eulogizers of Japan—Edmond de Goncourt, Pierre Loti, and above all the major artists of the day, from van Gogh to Monet via Manet and Toulouse-Lautrec— were succeeded by Paul Claudel, who had recently become a friend of the Cartier family. A writer as well as diplomat, Claudel had left his ambassadorial post in Tokyo two years earlier, where he had written one of his masterpieces, *The Satin Slipper*. His stay there inspired other books, including a fine volume of essays (*L'Oiseau noir dans le soleil levant*) and two "literary objects" (*Cent phrases pour éventails* and *Le vieillard sur le Mont Omi*, a text written on folded paper). No one in the Cartier family then realized that four years later little Marion, the daughter of Pierre Cartier, who headed the New York branch, would marry Pierre Claudel, son of the great writer who had become ambassador to the United States after leaving Tokyo. Marion was already attending the same school as the new ambassador's daughter, and the two families began seeing each other in 1928.

In 1936, Claudel would publish—in addition to a kind of ode to precious gems which the Cartiers would read prior to publication—one of the finest texts ever written on pens, inspired once again by Japan. "Japanese legend recounts that a certain woodcutter, on returning home with his axe on his shoulder, saw a strange light coming from the knots of a bamboo shoot and saw that this hermetic vessel served as a case enclosing a fairy. The same thing happened to me with my pen . . . It is a whole poem under pressure, it is a whole part of a book, it is a whole neighborhood of images and ideas that I keep bottled up, with no other outlet than this thread issuing from the end of the noncorroding nib, from the bottom of the ebonite cartridge. It is not surprising that an obscure complicity has arisen between this acute, spirit-filled finger and the three purely carnal ones that hold and guide it. Sometimes this rig leads me on . . . sometimes it becomes awkward and unhappy between my digits. It becomes bored, inattentive, distorting my designs, refusing to go where I want it to" ("Ossement," *Figures et Paraboles*).

PRECEDING PAGES: This Chinese-style **desk set** (1928)
is composed of an oval agate tray (20 x 15 cm)
with inkwell, dip pen with holder, and bowls for wiping
and drying the pen. The set is in black and red lacquer
on silver mountings, trimmed with coral and agate.

THIS PAGE: Design for a **nephrite blotter** (1925),
topped by a "Fo" dog on an oval amethyst base with
a trefoil pattern of rose-cut diamonds. Pencil, gouache
and watercolor on tracing paper. Cartier Archives.
Design for a **paper knife** (1930) of silver and black
lacquer with gold bands, its handle formed by a jade
Chinese fish with cabochon rubies for eyes. Pencil,
ink and gouache on tracing paper. Cartier Archives.

RIGHT: Author **Paul Claudel** (seen here in 1930,
when French ambassador to the United States) was
a friend of the Cartier family even before his son Pierre
married Marion Cartier. In 1936 Claudel wrote a fine
text on pens, based on a Japanese legend.

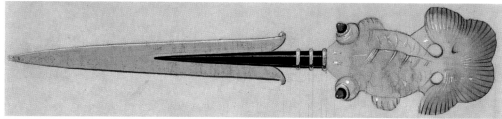

Perhaps Claudel mentioned this Japanese legend to the Cartiers. Whatever the case, the very year his text appeared—1936—the jewelers produced writing instruments in gold and bamboo: a fountain pen and mechanical pencil that became very popular. Bamboo, a Taoist yang symbol of power and virility (suggested by the rapid growth of bamboo, which reaches mature height in a matter of weeks), was a constant decorative motif of chinoiserie and Japonism. In addition to bamboo's appealing beauty and power, its longevity, sturdiness, and relatively ergonomic shape made it an ideal—and original— material for writing implements. Whether due to the virile symbolism or not, it was Cartier's female clients in particular who snatched up these graceful yet simple articles. There was even love at first sight between this new model and Daisy Decazes, one of the most elegant socialites of the day and wife of the Honorable Reginald Fellowes. Often proclaimed the best-dressed woman in the world, this Cartier client (as well as neighbor and friend) invented the sequined tuxedo-style jacket, and above all liked to be known for her highly studied simplicity, just like a true dandy. On December 14, 1936, Daisy bought a bamboo and gold dip pen, with gold cap and nib, and a matching mechanical pencil. The next day, she returned to buy a second bamboo pencil. And the following February 3rd found her at rue de la Paix once more, this time taking delivery of a third bamboo pencil featuring a gold snake-style chain. In 1936 and 1937, Princess Amarg of Kapurthala also bought three. Mrs. Cole Porter, Marlene Dietrich, and the duchess of Windsor, in turn, would also fall under bamboo's simple yet refined spell. The model would be reissued, entirely of gold, in 1956 and again in 1970. Having become highly prized by collectors, Cartier "bamboos" are now turning up in glamorous auctions.

The late 1930s were hounded by fear—the Roaring Twenties seemed a long way away. Anxiety at a threat which already seemed inevitable prompted a retreat to reliable, familiar values. Writing was one of them, for it allowed silent communication with loved ones. At Cartier, sales of fountain pens (still stubbornly labeled in French as "pens with ink reservoirs") were better than ever. In addition to the famous bamboo model, the firm successfully marketed a pen in polished gold endowed with a fine two-gold nib, a pressure filling system and a visible ink level. It also presented its first Waterman pen with cartridge (of glass, since rubber cartridges did not appear until 1954). It was

LEFT: Two Chinese-style **inkwells** with **pens** (1927). Top, the inkwell is set in a gray jade Chinese vase, its lid endowed with a rock-crystal ring. The vase handles are set with cabochon corals on which the gold and jet pen can rest. Bottom, a gray jade inkwell with an onyx lid, itself topped by carved carnelian decoration and a jade ball; the onyx base features two jade monkeys holding the onyx and carnelian pen. Cartier Archives.

FOLLOWING PAGES: **Marlene Dietrich**, whose artfully androgynous image constituted a perfect icon of the modern woman, seen in 1938 wearing a Cartier wristwatch. The same year, she bought a bamboo-style fountain pen from Cartier. Cartier had launched fountain pens and mechanical pencils made from real bamboo in 1936, with instant success. The bamboo motif was later revived in chased gold versions, as seen in this 1970 ballpoint pen. PAGES 106-7: Various **bamboo models** dating from 1938 to 1960. Note the two versions of the large model (27 cm), especially the one with two leads of different colors, sold in the 1950s. Cartier Archives.

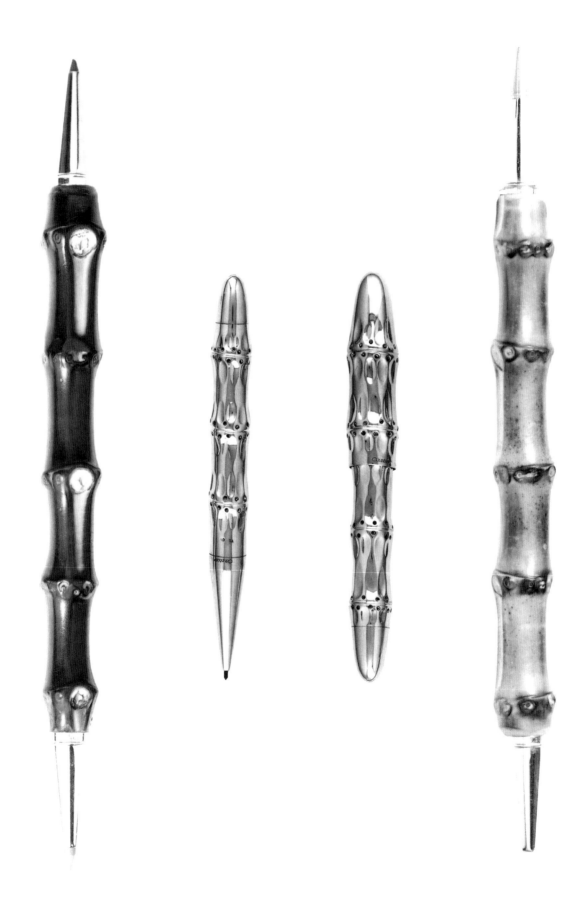

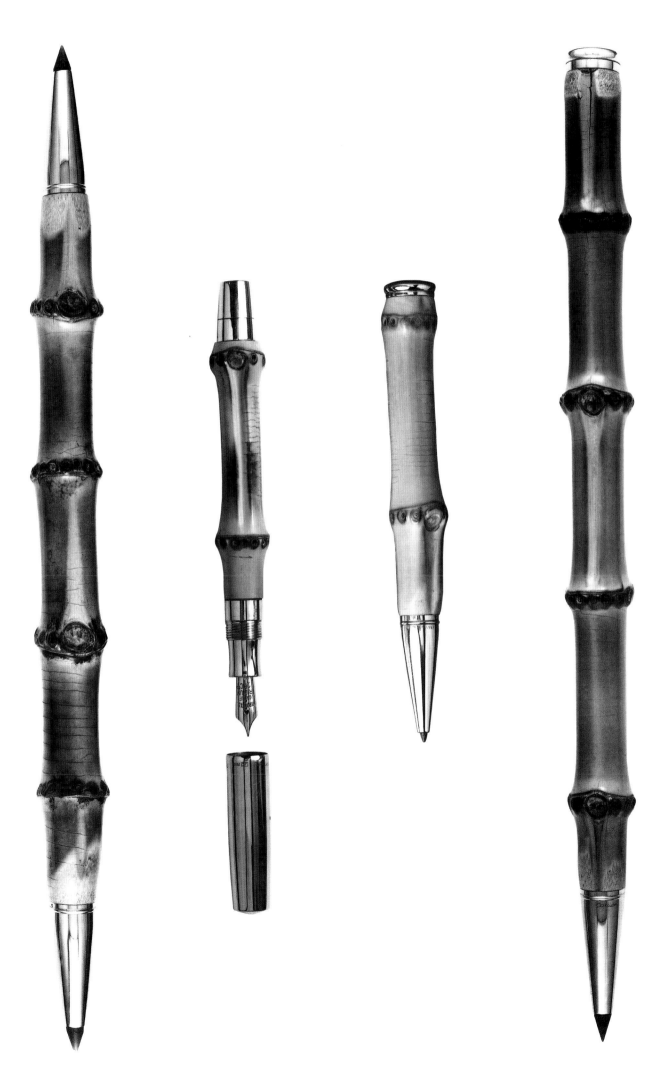

Design for an **inkwell** of aventurine and lapis lazuli (1928), marrying the colors green and blue (a favorite combination of Louis Cartier). Cartier Archives.

RIGHT: Cartier made this very pure octagonal **inkwell** (1928) of nephrite, endowed with an aventurine cover with yellow gold trim; the nephrite and yellow gold dip pen rests on an aventurine stand. Cartier Archives.

FOLLOWING PAGES: This sophisticated **desk set** (1928) features an electric buzzer activated by two agate buttons. In the middle is an inkwell on a green and black lacquer base with black lacquer lid crowned by a cabochon agate. It is flanked by gray agate bowls that serve as pen dryer and pen wiper. The dip pen and mechanical pencil are of agate, jet, and green enamel. Cartier Archives.

This **mechanical pencil** with built-in flashlight (*below*) designed to write in the dark, was bought in 1934 by the elegant Noel Coward, photographed in Paris by Horst the same year, wearing a Cartier watch (p. 112). A button on the tip turns on the light inside a 1930s **pencil-and-flashlight** combination in fluted silver and plastic. Art de Cartier Collection (p. 113). L E F T: Cartier produced several gold cases for cigarettes or calling cards which were personalized in the form of a stamped envelope with engraved address. Shown here is a **cigarette case** Cartier made in 1932 for Randolph Churchill, the 21-year-old journalist son of Winston.

Waterman's French importer, the JIF company, that had the brilliant idea of an ink cartridge, which was first marketed in 1936. Other writing instruments benefited from technical improvements, some of which were quite surprising: a fluted silver mechanical pencil was fitted with a tiny flashlight on the tip, for writing in the dark (the famous actor and writer Noel Coward, who scripted *Brief Encounter*, bought one at Cartier London in 1934). Meanwhile, Josephine Baker, one of the queens of the Roaring Twenties in Paris where she had been adored ever since she danced half-naked in the *Revue Nègre* of 1925, bought a simple but elegant eight-sided mechanical pencil in polished gold on November 26, 1937. A few days later, November 30th, her wedding day, she presented it to her beloved husband, Jean Lion; in a few years Baker would don the uniform of a second lieutenant in the Free French airforce. Finally, in 1939, the rage for animal motifs on objets d'art translated into a little ladybug of black enamel, set with brilliants, perched on a Cartier pen, thereby providing some final, frivolous glitter before darkness fell.

CHAPTER IV

Modern Times,

Modern Pleasures

During the dark days of war, the House of Cartier—unlike many other French companies—resolutely chose the path of freedom and honor. Louis Cartier emigrated to the United States where he died in 1942 after several years of illness. Jeanne Toussaint remained in occupied Paris, valiantly trying to deal with the difficulties: many of her colleagues had fled or were imprisoned, the main workshop was closed, and the store operated on limited stocks. "The panther" didn't balk at making her sympathies known, and was summoned to German headquarters after having ostentatiously displayed in the shop window a magnificent caged bird, symbolizing occupied France (it was blue, white, and red—lapis lazuli, diamonds, and coral—and began to sing when the cage door was opened). In London, the Cartier sales director, Étienne Bellanger, became part of General de Gaulle's circle. As soon as the general arrived in London in 1940, Bellanger provided him with a car and office premises, and frequently invited De Gaulle to dine at his house in Putney. When the Liberation came, Cartier sold pens and paper knives decorated with the Free-French Cross of Lorraine; Churchill perhaps saw one in the London shop when he purchased two pens there in May 1945.

In France, not everyone was delighted with the Liberation. The purge that followed put thousands of people in prison, too many of them innocent. Sacha Guitry, the undisputed king of French theater who had written some 100 plays and had recently begun making inspired movies, was himself arrested on August 23, 1944. He was accused of having been an active collaborator, based on the fact that his plays were often performed during the occupation; he had also accepted official posts as head of both the theater artists' association and the theater directors' organization. Guitry spent two months in an internment camp in Drancy, outside of Paris. Released prior to trial, his bank accounts were blocked and his plays banned; he found himself in financial straits, and was obliged to sell some paintings—including a Cézanne, a Monet, and a van Dyck—for a quarter of their value. He also got down to work again. Guitry, a narcissistic Don Juan and a fount of misogynistic wit, began to write what was intended to be a wonderfully spirited meditation on couples, titled *Elles et toi* ("Ladies and You"). In April 1945, while composing such one-liners as "Lying to women should be fun—it's like getting a refund" and "Sleep was the deepest thing about her," Guitry met the beautiful and

General de Gaulle photographed by Cecil Beaton in his London office during the war. Even as Jeanne Toussaint was openly defying the German occupiers in Paris, De Gaulle received the backing of Cartier executives in London. PRECEDING PAGE: Cartier cultivates tradition: in 1999 a new ballpoint model of the venerable **pen-calendar-watch combination** was launched, in black lacquer and gold plate. One year later, a black lacquer and platinum-finish version appeared; both versions were produced in limited editions of 2,000.

Cartier's **smaller fountain pens**, intended primarily for female clients, have always been very popular. This one of polished gold with projecting coral band, measures some ten centimeters long. **Sacha Guitry** (photographed here in 1954 on the set of *Affaires in Versailles*) bought a similar one in 1946 (with a band of lapis lazuli), probably as a gift for Lana Marconi. Art de Cartier Collection.

mysterious Lana Marconi. No one knew where she came from or how she made a living. Her mother was supposedly a Romanian actress, and rumor had it that Lana was the daughter of King Carol—which she didn't deny. Guitry would make her his wife (his fifth, and last) and a movie actress ("he could get a chair to act," quipped the great actress Pauline Carton). For the moment, though, he was still married to actress Geneviève de Séréville, and divorce proceedings were dragging on. On December 28, 1945, Sacha and Lana made a written vow to wed in the near future. The divorce was granted on February 13th, and on March 26th the sales staff on rue de la Paix saw Guitry enter the shop. The great playwright asked to see evening bags, then lipstick holders, then finally changed his mind: nothing would please Lana more than an object that would flatter her intelligence rather than her beauty. He bought a very elegant lady's pen of polished gold, adorned with a magnificent band of lapis lazuli.

Guitry would be acquitted, his case dismissed in 1947. He married Lana in 1949 and died in 1957. The 1950s in France were a time of painful reconstruction, and the luxury trade languished. During such difficult times, even wealthy clients—whether old or

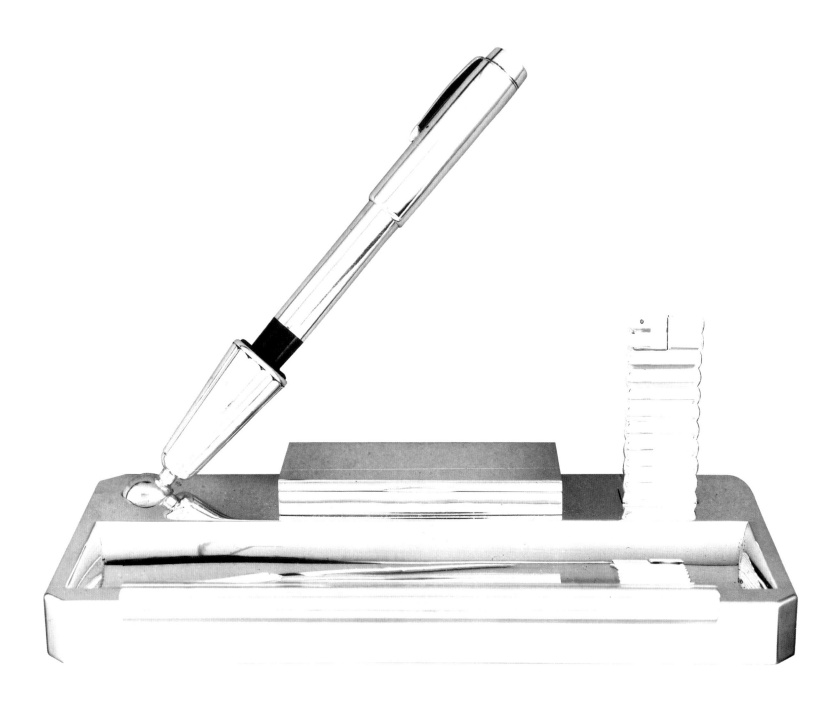

nouveau riche—were wary of flaunting a lavish lifestyle. Only a few privileged individuals and unchallenged aristocrats, such as the duke and duchess of Windsor, Ali Aga Khan and his half-brother Sadruddin, and Barbara Hutton dared to make glamorous purchases. In London, the Queen Mother commissioned a diamond tiara from Cartier in 1953; more modestly, at Christmas 1951 her son King George VI purchased as gifts a dozen silver mechanical pencils with case and two refills. There were few creative innovations in the realm of writing implements in those days. In 1960, Cartier presented an old-style gold dip pen set with two rows of brilliants. In fact, the firm concentrated on adorning the great classic pens made by the likes of Waterman (with a finely guilloched gold barrel), Shaeffer, and Parker. Cartier also sold the famous Parker 51, designed by Lazlo Moholy-Nagy, one of the driving forces behind the New Bauhaus in Chicago, who endowed this pen with the first non-screw cap and nearly invisible sheathed nib. The model enjoyed considerable popularity—fifty million were sold throughout the world!

Cartier excelled at embellishing pens made by others, as though the company's prodigious creativity was awaiting better days. In fact, everyone knew that nothing would ever be the same after the war, following the deaths of both Louis and Jacques in 1942. Great upheavals took place in the family firm. Louis's son Claude became president of Cartier New York, but sold the establishment in 1962. Marion Cartier, daughter of Pierre (who retired in 1947) sold the Paris branch in 1966, along with the Monte-Carlo and Cannes stores (which had opened before the war). Two years later, Jeanne Toussaint began to withdraw from the scene. These internal upheavals were accompanied by great changes in social attitudes during the 1960s. In the United States, Japan, Germany, Italy, and France, students rebelled against the establishment more or less violently. People protested about the war in Vietnam, the exploitation of others, hierarchical structures, middle-class morality. Trotskyists and Maoists worked toward a proletarian revolution, while other people advocated pacifism, free love and soft drugs, and still others sought a path between those two trends. Parallel to the violence of a handful of individuals and the hippie ethic of a few others, the generally rebellious atmosphere reflected and hastened profound changes occurring throughout society. Hypocritical

PRECEDING PAGES: Two silver **desk sets** from the 1940s. The pen stands, with fully pivoting holders, also boast a removable lighter and cigarette case. Note the subtle harmony of the bold, geometric reeding—horizontal, vertical, diagonal. Cartier Archives.
RIGHT: A few extremely precious writing accessories were produced by Cartier in the late 1940s, such as this gold mechanical pencil (1947) with lattice motif in rose-cut diamonds. A threaded push rod advances the lead.

When elected to the Académie Française in 1955, **Jean Cocteau**—a friend of Louis Cartier since the 1920s—designed his own dress sword, which Cartier then made. The handle depicts the poet Orpheus with his lyre; the column symbolizes the theater, the pen and paintbrush symbolize art. Cartier has made swords for some twenty academicians, including André Maurois and Maurice Druon. FOLLOWING PAGES: **Guilloche-work** is a great Cartier tradition. Here, studies for guilloche decoration on a gold Waterman pen (1953). Cartier began decorating certain models by leading pen manufacturers back in 1910. Cartier Archives.

128

Cartier

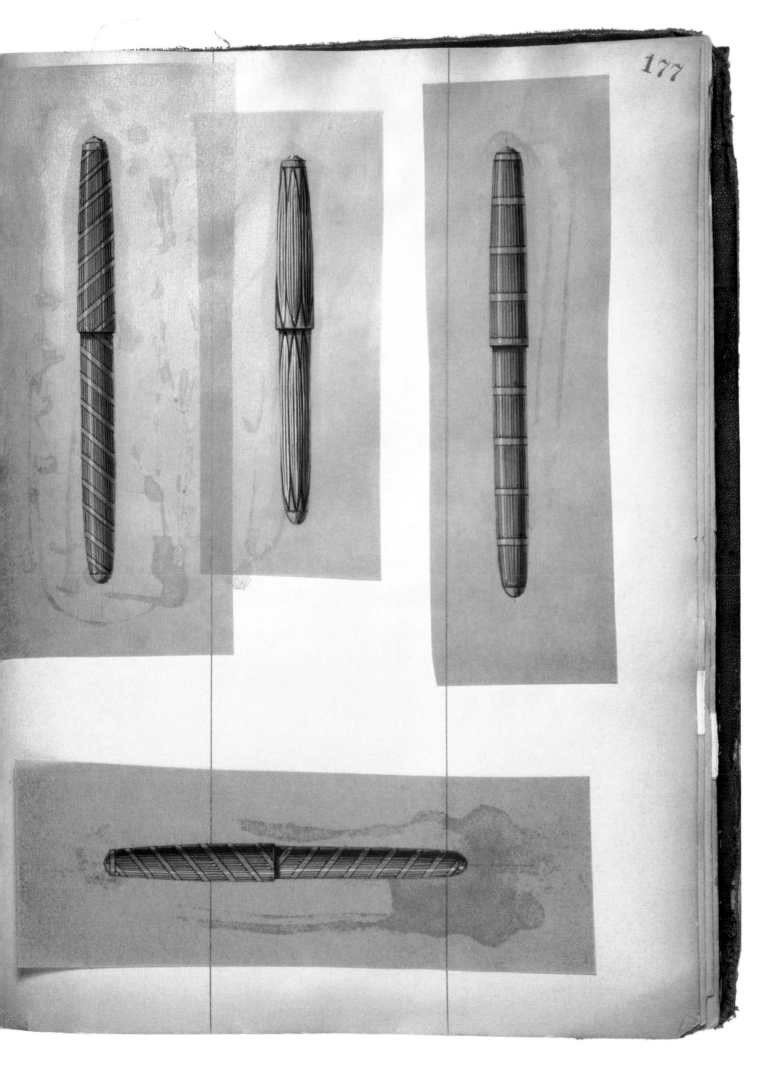

ABOVE: Two mechanical pencils from the late 1940s displaying intricate guilloche decoration. RIGHT: The gold-plated **Must pens** boast various costly finishes— reeding, guilloche patterning, etc. PRECEDING PAGES: Reeding is another traditional Cartier decoration. A special workshop fashions objects such as this reeded **gold ballpoint** (1972) set with a cabochon sapphire. Art de Cartier Collection.

morality, overly strict discipline, and rigid conventions were replaced by greater dialogue and harmony in interpersonal relationships. Feminist movements had never been so radical, and women were the first to benefit from the shift in attitudes. The world was changing once again. And once again, Cartier would change along with it.

❦

Cartier's revival occurred under the aegis of a visionary business man, Robert Hocq, who firmly believed in the luxury trade as long as it adapted to the times. He realized that whereas only a tiny elite would henceforth be attracted to pure finery—luxury for luxury's sake, luxury in and of itself—every year a growing number of men and women of taste were seeking objects that were handsome, impeccable, valuable, and functional all at once. He had headed a company that mass-produced lighters, Silver Match, and had always dreamed of the cigarette lighter he could produce if a great jeweler would grant him a license. Hocq had already designed this sublime lighter whose oval form displayed extremely pure, fine lines. Cartier was approached, was convinced, and soon signed a licensing agreement. In 1968, the Cartier lighter was launched. So great was its success that three years later, when a group of investors acquired control of Cartier Paris, Hocq was named president. From that point onward, the new president applied the same strategy to other functional items. After lighters came watches. But Hocq, quite rightly, was thinking big. If Cartier's modern luxury trade were to become accessible, then it should be everywhere, be highly visible, and easily identifiable. It needed a recognizable name and sales outlets throughout the world: the "Musts de Cartier" thus became both a product line and a chain of boutiques. Four initial shops were opened in Paris (Place Vendôme), Biarritz, Milan, and Singapore. Ten years later, they numbered one hundred.

The Musts de Cartier gave new creative impetus to the sphere of writing tools. It was henceforth an entire team that took charge of designing products which would reflect the needs of consumers and trends of the moment even as they remained strongly rooted in the Cartier identity, spirit, and history. Those two requirements resulted in items that soon became landmarks as Cartier steadily forged a reputation as a major pen designer. In 1976, after four years of planning, the first modern Cartier pen

was launched, an oval model called Vendôme de Cartier. Naturally, it was a ballpoint—Cartier ultimately had to react to the enormous popularity of ballpoint pens. The ballpoint was a French invention, patented in 1933 and perfected by the Hungarian brothers Ladislav and Georg Biro; it was marketed in 1945 by the American company Reynolds, and finally made famous the world over by the French baron Michel Bich, who invented the universal, disposable "Bic." In 1958, the baron bought Waterman and, seven years later, French children were authorized to use ballpoints at school. The future of fountain pens seemed to be darkened forever. In fact, though, they would dawn again thanks to inexpensive models made of plastic.

The Vendôme de Cartier ballpoint was a magnificent gold-plated object, oval in shape like the lighter, with a burgundy lower section, decorated with three interlaced bands recalling one of the firm's historic emblems, the trinity ring. Particularly striking was the pen's patented, retractable clip: pressing the top triggered a clockwork mechanism that pushed a lateral clip to the extent desired—releasing the pressure eased the clip gently on the pocket or returned it to its housing. The pen was officially launched in the grandiose setting of Taormina, Sicily, whose archaeological ruins reflected the pen's "column" look. The magnificent party organized that day marked the start of a new promotional strategy for Cartier, perfectly adapted to its special new image: a subtle combination of the classical and the spectacular, of elegance and boldness. The pen was a hit, and in subsequent years the firm's designers developed a solid silver version of the oval pen, decorated with four different guilloche patterns. The three rings were silver gilt. In September 1979, a variant previously thought impossible due to the pen's oval form was finally ready—a fountain pen.

The firm's design workshops, which also developed watches, leather goods, eyeglasses, and perfumes, became a hotbed of activity. In 1983, the infatuation with the Vendôme de Cartier was still going strong when a completely new line of pens was introduced, simply dubbed "Musts." This decision to present simultaneously, under a now-famous name, all four modes of writing—fountain pen, ballpoint, felt-tip, and pencil—was an event in itself. The press described the move as more than just dynamic, perceiving it as a bold risk, especially since the implements represented a radical break

The first writing implement in the Must de Cartier line was the **oval ballpoint pen** adorned with the traditional trinity ring (1976). The firm's design department then spent three years reconciling the flattened shape with the ink-feed for a fountain pen, and in 1979 the ballpoint was joined by the oval fountain pen (ultimately offered in twenty decorative versions). Shown here are two pens, one with horizontal reeding, the other in lacquer.

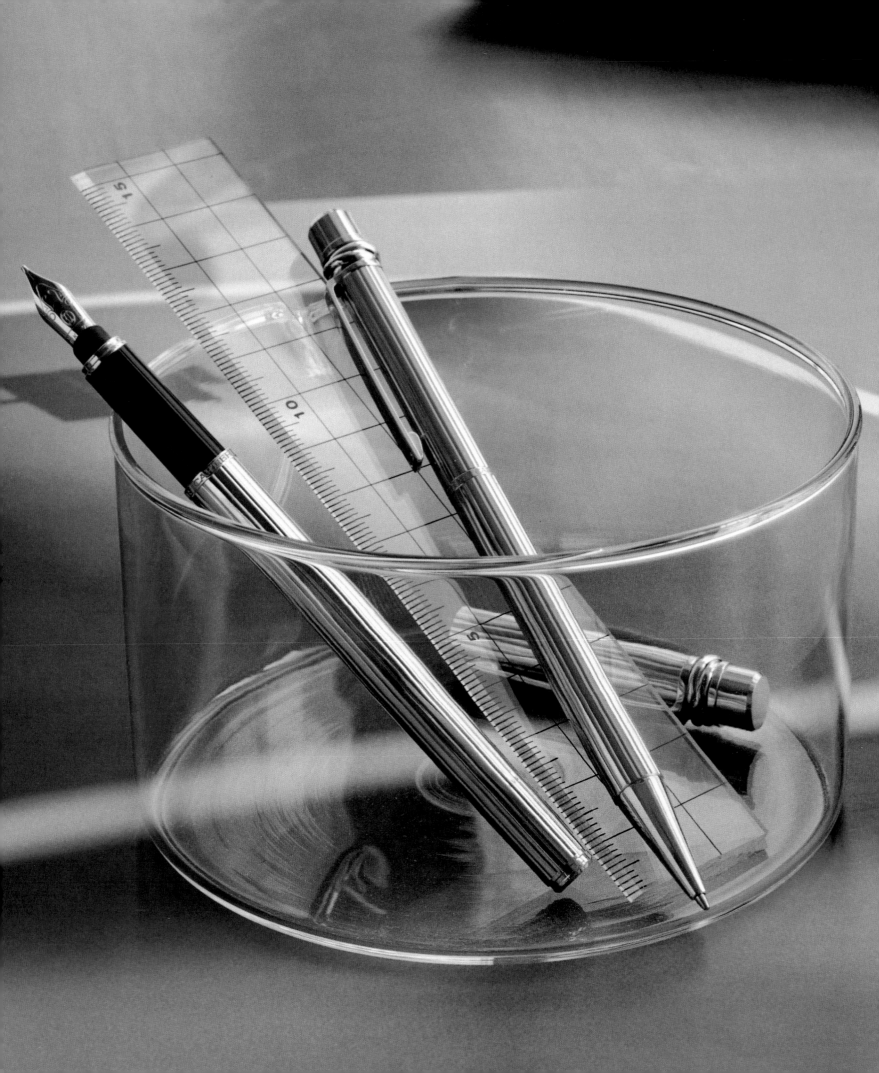

with the highly identifiable oval image of the Vendôme de Cartier—the Must pens were a more functional tubular shape. Risk-taking, however, was very much in the air at that time, and was synonymous with high performance. The press release for the launch of the line, for that matter, was typical of the 1980s in its stress on the "high-performance" aspect of the Musts. In fact, the striking simplicity of the name and shape of the pens was naturally designed to serve as a straightforward setting that would underscore luxurious decoration and lavish customizing: Must pens were magnificently dressed in lacquer, silver, or 23-carat gold; various colors of lacquer were offered, and some magnificent gold versions were decorated along the sides with motifs recalling bamboo or lattice-work. The Cartier image became sharper and firmer—alongside the traditional reeding (called "vertical godrons"), trinity rings, and intertwined-C monogram, there appeared a finely chased solid 18-carat gold pen marked with the double C. A new, patented hinged clip was developed with an even more ingenious pivot system. In addition to these refinements worthy of a great jeweler, Cartier offered another major attraction for all lovers of the art of writing—a choice of nibs (four widths), ballpoints (two sizes), and ink (blue, black, or burgundy). Nearly twenty years later, the timeless Must line still exists. The fountain pens now come in a fifth size (extra large), and customers can choose between the trinity ring or the sportier Santos ring with its three small screws, inspired by the watch of the same name. Wedded to a steel barrel, this model evoked a great moment in the Cartier legend.

Yet perhaps it was more than an evocation or tribute. By the 1980s, it seemed that the firm's designers were focusing on marrying a strong historical image to newly sensual shapes and materials. Platinum, a fascinating metal delightful to caress, would resurface at the end of the 1990s, while lacquer—soft and silky to the feel—had already returned in 1986 on a highly sensual pen named Pasha. This very valuable pen reflected a shift in attitudes: nearly fifteen years after the Musts de Cartier were launched, it seemed that something had changed in the way luxury items were perceived. Precious materials and objects had once again found favor among the public. They not only represented know-how that needed to be preserved and protected, but also a source of highly skilled jobs in times of uncertain employment. Glamorous brands thus enjoyed

PRECEDING PAGES: The pens dubbed "Musts" appeared in 1983. Once again, Cartier offered clients a wide range of decorative models. The **lacquer series**, in particular, came in an impressive range of tones and patterns—bark, malachite, blue-gray or green marble, lapis, Veronese, cobalt, burgundy, blue or gray jasper, flamboyant. Cartier's lacquer workshop, with a hospital-like sterile environment, jealously keeps its production methods secret. Up to forty coats of lacquer are sometimes required. LEFT: The new **Must de Cartier pens**—a fountain pen and a gold-plated ballpoint with vertical reeding and the trinity ring trademark.

renewed popularity—their names were proudly displayed on the body. Soon this enthusiasm became a veritable infatuation with designer names, winning over young people from every walk of life. Thus it is hardly surprising that in 1986 Cartier also returned to a certain concept of luxury in the design of certain items. The Pasha, whose name evoked both oriental splendors and powerful men, came in a veritable jewelry case and was produced in a limited edition. Each one received forty layers of burgundy or black lacquer (a magnificent blue version would be issued shortly afterward). The pen's rounded forms suggested the 1930s, and its cap was of reeded gold plate, decorated with the trinity ring on which the production number and year were etched. Above all, it was crowned with a cabochon onyx or ruby, thus marking the return of the most luxurious emblem of Cartier writing implements since their origins. To complete this rebirth of lavishness, in 1989 the pen was joined by an oval-shaped crystal inkwell marked with the double C in fine gold. The inkwell accompanied the arrival of a new refilling mechanism that made it possible to draw ink from a well, which users could themselves insert in place of the cartridge. For the ever-growing number of nostalgics, this "converter" would henceforth be offered on all fountain pens. At a time when typewriters had long been king and word-processing software was already appearing on computers, Cartier sensed the nostalgia for a golden age of penmanship with all its attendant paraphernalia.

The success of the elitist Pasha spurred Cartier to go one step further—why not offer a specially commissioned pen, as was done in the days of fantastic fortunes? Such pens would be known either as Signature Pasha (featuring the client's signature etched in gold on the lacquer) or Precious Pasha (of solid gold, with a cap studded with diamonds and sapphires). These highly exclusive items had to be ordered six months in advance, and were aimed at a clientele that Cartier, faithful to its century-old principles, wanted to continue to serve. The firm's designers nevertheless kept their feet on the ground. In 1991, there appeared an upscale pen that was more affordable and above all more evocative of the Cartier legend: the Panthère pen. This subtly spotted model came in four versions: black lacquer and gold, jasper blue lacquer and gold, reeded silver, and reeded gold. It also featured Cartier's two trademarks, a trinity ring and a cabochon onyx

The limited-edition **Pasha** was unveiled in 1986. With its lacquer barrel, reeded gold cap, trinity ring, and colorful cabochon, this pen combines all the main Cartier emblems in an elegant manner.

or sapphire. The pen, aimed primarily at a female clientele, accompanied an entire range of accessories evoking the panther. This animal was emblematic of several decades of Cartier's history, having been the mascot of the mysterious and flamboyant Jeanne Toussaint. Back in 1914 already, a spotted panther pattern appeared on a pendant-watch. In 1917, it was the entire animal—of onyx and brilliants—that featured in relief on a Cartier vanity case made for Toussaint herself. This vanity case was the first in a long series of panthers. Much later, in the 1940s, the duchess of Windsor, Barbara Hutton, and Daisy Fellowes wore panther or tiger brooches designed by Cartier. Ten years later, a new fan of this design became a regular Cartier customer, namely Nina Dyer. Born in Ceylon, the daughter of an English tea planter, Dyer was a ravishingly beautiful former model who first married Baron Henri Thyssen-Bornemiza and later Prince Sadruddin Aga Khan, son of Aga Khan III. For Dyer, Cartier designed in 1957 an extraordinary panther set composed of a stick pin, an articulated brooch, a ring, and two bracelets. The second bracelet was a tour-de-force that would go down in jewelry history: the two panther heads on the ends could be removed to be worn as earrings or set on an evening bag whose handle was formed by the main part of the bracelet. The strong personality and legendary associations of the Panthère pen struck the public, which snapped up the item. Cartier immediately launched a masculine version, called the Cougar, which imitated the Panthère's feline form but eliminated the spots, being soberly dressed in reeded silver plating with anthracite details.

Two years later, in 1993, the tenth anniversary of Must pens called for a worthy celebration: the House of Cartier startled people once again by offering a new generation of pens, called Must II. Never had Cartier designed so pure and simple an object. The ballpoints with their resolutely straight barrels, devoid of the henceforth classic attributes of triple ring and cabochon, decorated solely with reeding or lacquer, clearly signaled the firm's goal of fulfilling every demand—not only a demand for finery and magnificence, but also the demand for simplicity and discretion. The need to assert tradition and heritage was combined with a desire—especially among a younger clientele—for a more understated image. As always, the common denominator remained an extreme concern for elegance, refinement, and outstanding quality. The Must II line

The **Panthère pen** was launched in 1991 as a tribute to Jeanne Toussaint and the entire "panther" tradition at Cartier. It came in several versions—lacquer, silver or gold. The spots are composed of onyx. The Panthère includes two key Cartier attributes: the trinity ring and a cabochon onyx or sapphire.

was therefore equipped with a high-tech rotating command mechanism and a highly sturdy self-springing clip, making eternal objects of these pens.

❦

For people who passionately enjoy writing by hand, 1995 will be remembered as the year Cartier launched a magical pen—the Louis Cartier. It spectacularly confirmed the jeweler's new determination to make pens that could rival its most glamorous competitors' top-level models in terms of writing quality and comfort. Thus in the mid-1990s Cartier truly became a specialist in top-quality pens, establishing a benchmark for the most demanding clients.

The Louis Cartier pen instantly came across as a masterpiece from both stylistic and technical standpoints. First of all, it was perfectly suited to its times. Even as new technology was increasingly invading everyday life in the form of microprocessors, the Internet, and genetic engineering, the 1990s turned to nostalgia as a sign of cultural authenticity. Never had writers, painters, and singers of the past been so popular. Never had retrospectives, commemorations, and "best of" compilations been so numerous. So, just as record companies not only resuscitated but also rejuvenated deceased performing artists via new remastering techniques, so Cartier's new pen appropriated the age-old symbol of writing, the quill pen, by endowing it with everything the latest technology could offer and adorning it in finery worthy of it. The new model would be a tribute to traditional pens and a tribute to Louis Cartier, a man of the past whose elegant, creative, and ever-rejuvenated spirit still inhabits 13 rue de la Paix and spans the globe. Flipping through Louis's own notebooks reveals that he was not only a great fan of drawings, but also of writing, which is why the 1995 pen was dubbed Louis Cartier. Entirely hand-worked in solid 18-carat gold, the hallmarked nib featured two-color decoration with a classic garland motif and the double C monogram. This elegantly "retro" look, however, housed a treasure of technical efficiency. Never have people written so well as with this Cartier in hand. Its iridium point allows it to glide matchlessly across the page, while its broad feed tube provides optimum ink flow to create optimum lines. It comes, of course, in five writing widths, instantly interchangeable thanks to the tried-and-tested system of screwable nib blocks.

The **Louis Cartier pen**, introduced in 1995, enthused connoisseurs with its incomparable writing quality as well as its rare elegance. No other pen writes so well. In 1996, as a tribute to ebonite (that extraordinary substance used in early-twentieth-century pens before it was dethroned by cheaper materials), Cartier launched a Louis Cartier model in brown ebonite in 1996, limited to 1,847 copies (the year the firm was founded). Two years later, a green ebonite version was unveiled. These rare, limited-edition pens are also adorned with an onyx-colored cabochon-cut spinel.

The nib block is the "nerve center" of every pen and requires dozens of hours of work and above all a great deal of skill on the part of various highly qualified artisans. The nib itself demands many minute operations, from the initial flattening of a gold ingot into a fine sheet which is cut to the correct pattern, pierced with an eye, given an iridium tip, split between eye and tip, and curved into the right shape, to subsequent hand-decorating with engraved arabesques and the double C monogram, to polishing and final checking for elasticity and caliber. The nib blocks, which include the nib itself and the ink feed, are then mounted on the pen by hand. Every pen is tested under actual writing conditions: lines in every direction (straight, curved, and signature movements) are made in blue ink, breaking in the pen and insuring that the nib block functions properly. Any nibs that catch the paper or leave gaps are immediately returned for a corrective polishing.

The Louis Cartier pen, whose rounded, 1930s shape feels very pleasant in the hand, is available either entirely in reeded gold, or in lacquer combined with reeded gold. Its cap also employs an amazing screw system used in clockmaking—the screwing action becomes tighter toward the finish thanks to a threaded ring of special steel (plated first in titanium, then in gold), which means that it cannot unscrew accidentally.

The Louis Cartier pen was crowned with a cabochon of black resin and stamped with a C on the clip. Later versions featured different finishes, including two world firsts: a reeded, black composite material produced by revolutionary technology which makes for an incredibly light pen; and a platinum finish, launched in 1998 as a tribute

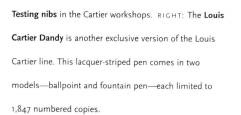

Testing nibs in the Cartier workshops. RIGHT: The **Louis Cartier Dandy** is another exclusive version of the Louis Cartier line. This lacquer-striped pen comes in two models—ballpoint and fountain pen—each limited to 1,847 numbered copies.

to a hundred-year-old tradition in the firm, which was the first to employ this most precious of metals. Ballpoint and rollerball versions of the Louis Cartier also exist. The latter comes equipped with an innovative "capless" refill which not only provides markedly longer writing time than conventional refills, but also prevents the ball from drying out if the cap is left off for several hours.

The timeless design of the Louis Cartier has also been the basis of a few limited editions, totalling 1,847 numbered pens (commemorating the year the firm was founded) known as Louis Cartier Dandies. In 1996, collectors were thrilled to discover the first series, in brown ebonite. It was the first time that a major brand re-employed this unusual material—a highly resistant, nonporous resin obtained from vulcanized rubber—which participated in the rise of fountain pens in the late nineteenth and early twentieth century, only to be abandoned. In 1998, Cartier presented a new version in green ebonite. The following year there appeared a Louis Cartier Dandy whose thin stripes of black lacquer set in the gold-plated barrel inevitably recalled the good old striped enamel of the precious dip pens of yore. And, as in the old days, each pen was an exclusive, crafted object.

Meanwhile, in 1997 Cartier celebrated its 150th anniversary. The event called for the designing of four outstanding models that were sold by subscription, just like any other edition of precious objects. Two were produced in only fifteen copies: a watch-pen in solid 18-carat yellow gold, oval in shape, decorated with lattice-work gold on lacquer; and a solid gold version of the Louis Cartier featuring the same decoration, with a crystal inkwell. The other two anniversary editions were produced in 150 copies: a solid 18-carat gold Louis Cartier pen with vertical reeding and a band decorated with an arabesque of black lacquer, also accompanied by a crystal inkwell; and a magnificent "mini-ballpoint" in gold reeding and a cap set with a cabochon sapphire.

The Louis Cartier pen appeared in two other highly exceptional versions. In 2000, the firm presented the Precious Louis Cartier pen in solid plain gold with a cap and cabochon studded with 823 brilliants, or in solid reeded gold with a cabochon sapphire or emerald plus a clip set either with a single emerald or with two emeralds and three sapphires. Finally, that same year, to celebrate the dawn of the third millennium in lavish

Produced by special order since 2000, this **Louis Cartier** may be the most valuable pen in the world. The solid-gold pen is studded with 823 full-cut diamonds weighing over 15.5 carats. No less than 350 hours go into crafting each one. FOLLOWING PAGES: Design and photo of an 18-carat **gold oval ballpoint** with watch, produced in fifteen copies on the occasion of Cartier's 150th anniversary. The cap is etched with the "150th-anniversary pattern" and the black lacquer barrel features the same pattern in yellow gold.

fashion, the House of Cartier chose the Louis Cartier line to innovate radically by launching a pen in which both barrel and nib were of platinum. Producing a platinum nib was a technical exploit, since this fairly rigid metal had to be specially worked to yield the necessary suppleness. The Platinum Louis Cartier is a new pen for a new world, a superlative pen made to last more than a thousand years thanks to a wonderful material rendering it both more valuable and more functional. With this pen, Cartier assumed its place in the history of writing.

That history has been written behind the scenes—or rather in the spotlights—of the firm's workshops. It is hard to appreciate the amount of instinct, creativity, and know-how that goes into the launching of a Cartier pen. From the moment a need is felt to the moment that need has been met, three or four years may pass—years of research, of development, of production. Take, for example, that hard-to-classify little wonder, the Diabolo de Cartier line, which is simultaneously modern yet classic, simple yet elegant, precious yet familiar. Whether fountain pen, ballpoint, rollerball or pencil, the Diabolo de Cartier is now the heart of the Cartier range, having been launched in 1997. And yet its history goes back to 1994. On March 1st of that year, after months of reflection, the firm decided to develop a new pen. The main goal was to reflect the growing interest, particularly among younger clients, for designed writing instruments with pure lines and sober appearance. Fashion in those years was dominated by austere lines and the color black, promoted by avant-garde Japanese clothes designers such as Yohji Yamamoto and the "Comme des Garçons" team. Artists and intellectuals throughout the world adopted black as a fashion statement. Ever aware of the prevailing mood, Cartier decided to explore that path, at the same time seeking to refine its jewelry tradition. So a whole new range of writing instruments was to be created—retractable pencils and ballpoints, fountains pens and rollerballs with caps. The objects had to be of composite material or lacquer, of the same length as the Must line but perhaps a little wider, with novel, more curved shapes. The firm's designers were free to incorporate the trinity ring or not. They nevertheless had to assert the Cartier personality clearly, all the while providing "innovative, even daring" decoration. The pen would be developed along the rough lines of the Louis Cartier range, though smaller.

In a worthy celebration of the third millennium, the year 2000 saw the unveiling of a special **all-platinum Louis Cartier** model. Its cabochon, set atop the reeded body, is a genuine onyx. FOLLOWING PAGES: Thanks to their pure, almost Art Deco lines and an instantly recognizable, low-slung clip (leaving the sapphire-colored cabochon always visible), **Diabolo de Cartier pens,** launched in 1997, immediately appealed to a young, urban, intellectual clientele. Left to right, part of the Diabolo de Cartier line: composite rollerball with platinum-finish attributes (clip and bands); composite ballpoint with gold-plated attributes; composite fountain pen with platinum-finish attributes; composite fountain pen with gold-plated attributes; mini mechanical pencil of composite material with platinum-finish attributes.

Some **preparatory drawings**. Left to right, the platinum-finish dip pen (see p. 161), two Diabolo de Cartier pens, and a ballpoint-calendar-watch pen (see p. 117).

RIGHT: A **Diabolo de Cartier fountain pen** in brushed steel with platinum-finish clip and bands.

The firm's designers studied all the requirements of the project, then got down to work. Early drawings were a long way from the final goal—sketches like absent-minded doodles made while chatting on the telephone. Little by little, however, this material shaped up into a few evocative lines, then an overall form. Over a number of days, this form became more precise—never to change. It was oblong, as desired, yet very pure, tapering toward the tip. Then came the details—clip, band, colors. This stage was the most interesting to observe, with designers bent over their tables in concentration, wielding their tools—pencils, super-fine sable brushes, tubes of gouache, squares, rulers, etc. In June 1994, after three months of work, three very different ballpoint proposals were submitted in the form of magnificent, life-sized drawings in gouache and

ink. The workshop's first proposal called for a pen with a rounded end, below which was the trinity ring, beneath which was placed a thin, curved clip; just before the gold lower section, there came a set of coral and gold bands. The second proposal was more sober: a pen with a flat end to which the clip was affixed, plus two bands of gold before a long lower section of purple completed by a gold tip. The third plan was simultaneously soberer and bolder: an Art Deco-style pen, entirely black, whose sole note of color (besides gold) was a blue cabochon on the end, ringed by two concentric bands of gold; a clip was attached by a band set very low, echoed by a single small band just before the tip. Even as various departments were studying these proposals, the design workshop went to work on the fountain pen. On September 30th, it submitted two designs, variants on the first two ballpoint proposals. On October 12th, the decision came—only the boldest design, with the blue cabochon, was accepted. A mock-up was made and presented to a small committee of three which assessed its technical feasibility—and rejected it. So over the next two years, constant collaboration between the various technical departments led to the refinement of every detail. At this point, decisions were being made down to the millimeter. The idea of positioning the clip lower, for instance, was adopted because it enabled the pen to be seen once placed in a pocket, becoming one of the distinctive marks of the Diabolo de Cartier. But it was above all the lower end and tip of the pen that took a long time to resolve; the band was finally abandoned in favor of a little gold tip, and the design for the nib was adopted in November 1996. Both fountain pen and ballpoint were finalized in January 1997 and a prototype was then made.

Finally production began. Even for a pen such as this, there was no question of industrial output. Tooling, electroplating, polishing and assembly are all subtle operations executed by roughly one hundred highly skilled artisans working for the firm.

Right from its launch, the Diabolo de Cartier—dressed all in black with a crown of blue, featuring simple, elegant yet highly novel lines—appealed to the young, urban clientele Cartier was seeking. It quickly became the best-selling upmarket pen. Rollerball and mechanical-pencil versions were soon added to the line, as well as new decorative details such as reeding and platinum finishes. Most of all, three "mini" Diabolos de Cartier in black and gold were offered to customers who preferred to hold—

The **Diabolo de Cartier** is also available in a reeded platinum-finish model.

and carry—a lighter, smaller object. The modern styling of the Diabolo de Cartier, combined with the glamorous series of Louis Cartier pens and the handsome, timeless refinement of the Must II, means that Cartier finally offered, for the first time in its history, a coherent range worthy of a great name in penmaking. And Cartier could trump that accomplishment with its trademark *stylos d'exception*, the "exclusive pens" that for over 150 years have made the jeweler's reputation and that now incorporate contemporary know-how. In 1999 and 2000, a wonderful object was issued in two limited editions of two thousand copies each, an object steeped in the firm's long tradition yet displaying high-tech features: a ballpoint-calendar-watch combination in elegant black lacquer and gold (one edition) or platinum (the other edition).

This outstanding object underscores once again Cartier's respect for its own tradition. This respect is also evident in the patient search and acquisition of old items made by the company since it was founded, thereby constituting the "Cartier Art Collection." The collection currently boasts over 1,200 pieces tracing the evolution in Cartier style and technology in terms both of highly precious jewelry and accessory items, some of the finest of which are writing implements. At the time of writing, the oldest is a 1906 mechanical pencil in the form of a feather, and the most recent is a 1977 paperweight adorned with "Snoopy" in platinum. These objects are not only preserved as precious works of art, but are also regularly exhibited to the public. Paper knives, fountain pens, dip pens and mechanical pencils, inkwells and notepads are thus displayed alongside the finest gems, appreciated by marveling visitors to the greatest museums in the world.

Meanwhile, Cartier has been designing pens for the third millennium—the solid platinum Louis Cartier, the new Must pen, and even a traditional dip pen! The Cartier of the third millennium seems to be coming full circle, showing that nothing can be created without a sense of heritage, tradition, and collective memory. Yet every modern convenience is added: the dip pen for the year 2000, with platinum finish and produced in just two thousand copies, features a special solid 18-carat gold calligraphic nib making it possible to write an entire page with just one dip in the well; yet it can also work with one of the five standard nib blocks, can take a cartridge or converter, and comes with a cap. In these days of e-mail and the Internet, Cartier is spectacularly defending

Limited to 2,000 copies destined for lovers of calligraphy and fine handwriting, this **traditional pen** works the "old fashioned way" (dipped into an inkwell) or with a cartridge or converter. It comes with either a standard nib or, as here, a calligraphic nib. The barrel and cap are reeded platinum finish. The profound pleasure of writing is rekindled by this new version of the dip pen.

the right to experience the delight of writing by hand on a sheet of paper. This pleasure is increasingly under threat, but should not be allowed to die. For that would mean abandoning one of mankind's most elegant and noble activities. Through handwriting, mankind has made the human body a most sophisticated tool as well as a great source of sensuality and grace. By reinventing the dip pen today, Cartier is stressing and celebrating the value of that activity. The jeweler is attempting to return, imaginatively, to the source of that pleasant sensation. Long buried yet never forgotten is the sensation of the tip of a pen moving to a very old waltz, the sound of a nib tapping the bottom of the well. For all those schoolchildren born before the 1960s, the sharp scent of ink can be relived at last. And younger people, finally, can now discover the intense pleasure of writing—preferably words of love, all perfumed with eternity.

Design for a spherical crystal inkwell and pen (circa 1930). Pencil, India ink, and gouache on tracing paper. Cartier Archives.

Acknowledgments

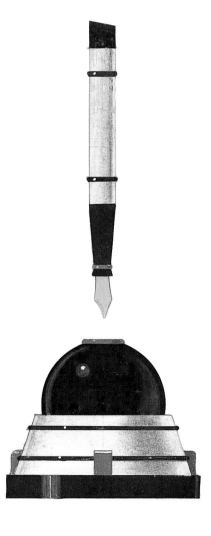

The author would like to extend warm thanks to all the people at Cartier whose help was invaluable during the writing of this book. Special thanks go to Betty Jais, archivist for haute joaillerie, who patiently guided his research and provided essential information for the captions. He wishes to acknowledge Franco Cologni and Suzanne Tise-Isoré, without whom this book would not have been possible. He is also grateful to connoisseur-collector Jean-Claude Colban and to social historian François L'Yvonnet, whose expertise and libraries greatly enriched these pages, and to Bernard Lagacé for his beautiful and thoughtful book design.

The publisher is grateful to all those at Cartier who provided so much time and material for the book: Richard Lepeu, Franco Cologni, Suzy Otéro, Eric Nussbaum, Pierre Rainero, Christine Borgoltz, Bernard Fornas, Nicolas Roux-Alezais, Jacques Diltoer, Florence Loiseleur, Grazia Valtorta, Marc Frisanco, Jean-Marie Guénot, Jérome Favier, Christopher Glick, Amélie Delcroix, Bonnie Selfe, Brian Jennings, Moya Corcoran, Maud Charasson, Alain Beaufort, Bernhard Berger, Anne-Christine Charbonnaz, Renée Frank, Véronique Sacuto, Michel Aliaga, Jacqueline Ronconi, Nathalie Ghatan.

We wish to thank the paper manufacturer Thiberge & Comar and the glassware supplier L. Rossignol for graciously lending materials used in the photographs.

Bibliography

On Writing

André-Salvine, Béatrice *et al.*, *L'ABCdaire des Écritures*,
  Paris: Flammarion, 2000.
Bonfante, Larissa, *La Naissance des écritures*, Paris:
  Le Seuil, 1994.
Boulanger, J.-P. *et al.*, *Naissance de l'écriture, cunéiformes
  et hiéroglyphes*, Paris: RMN, 1982.
Calvet, Louis-Jean, *Histoire de l'écriture*, Paris: Plon, 1996.
Cohen, Marcel, *La Grande invention de l'écriture
  et son évolution*, Paris: Imprimerie Nationale, 1958.
Diringer, David, *Writing*, New York: Praeger, 1962.
Druet, Roger, and Herman, Grégoire, *La Civilisation
  de l'écriture*, Paris: Fayard, 1976.
Février, James G., *Histoire de l'écriture*, Paris: Payot, 1948.
Gaur, Albertine, *A History of Writing*, London:
  British Library, 1984.
Harris, Roy, *The Origin of Writing*, La Salle (Ill.):
  Open Court, 1986.
Higounet, Charles, *L'Écriture*, Paris: PUF, 1955.
Jean, Georges, *L'Écriture mémoire des hommes*, Paris:
  Gallimard, 1987.
Naveh, Joseph, *Early History of the Alphabet*, Jerusalem:
  Magnes Press, 1982.
Pulver, Max, *Le Symbolisme de l'écriture*, Paris: Stock, 1971.

On Writing Implements

Doisy, Marie-Ange, and Fulacher, Pascal, *Papiers et moulins*,
  Paris: Technorama, 1989.
Dragoni, Giorgio, and Fichera, Giuseppe, *Stylos:
  De l'écriture à la collection*, Paris: Gründ, 1998.
Fischler, G., and Schneider, S., *Fountain Pens & Pencils,
  The Golden Age of Writing Instruments*, West Chester
  (Pa.): Schiffer Publishing, 1990.
Geyer, Dietmar, *Collecting Writing Instruments*,
  West Chester (Pa.): Schiffer Publishing, 1990
Guéno, J.-P., Lussato, B., and Tatsuno, K., *Un amour
  de stylo*, Paris: Musée de la Poste/Robert Laffont, 1995
Haury, Pierre, and Lacroux, Jean-Pierre, *Une affaire
  de stylos*, Paris: Seghers, 1990.
Jansley, June, *The Collector's Book of Ink Bottles*,
  Bembridge, 1976.
Lacroux, Jean-Pierre, and Van Cleem, Lionel, *La Mémoire
  des Sergent-Major*, Paris: Ramsay, 1988.
Lambrou, Andreas, *Fountain Pens, Vintage and Modern*,
  London: Sotheby's, 1989.

Lawrence, Cliff, *Fountain Pens*, Paducah (Ky.):
  Collector Books, 1977.
Le Collen, Éric, *Objects d'écriture*, Paris: Flammarion, 1998.
Margival, F. *Les encres*, Paris: Gauthiers Villars-Mason, 1912.
Pernoud, Régine and Vigne, Jean, *La Plume et le parchemin*,
  Paris: Denoël 1983.
Weing, Alexander Crum, *Le stylo à plume, guide
  du collectionneur*, Courbevoie (Fr.): Soline, 1997.

On Cartier

Barraca, J., Negretti, G., and Nencini, F., *Le Temps
  de Cartier* (with English text), Milan: Publi Prom, 1993.
Cologni, Franco and Mochetti, Ettore, *Made by Cartier:
  150 Years of Tradition and Innovation*, Paris/Lausanne:
  Bibliothèque des Arts, 1992.
Cologni, Franco and Nussbaum, Eric, *Platinum by Cartier*,
  New York: Abrams, 1996.
Gautier, Gilberte, *La saga des Cartier*, Paris: Michel Lafon,
  1998.
Nadelhoffer, Hans, *Cartier Jewelers Extraordinary*, London:
  Thames and Hudson, 1984.
Rudoe, J., *Cartier 1900-1939*, New York: Abrams, 1997.
Tretiack, P., *Cartier*, Paris: Assouline, 1996.

Picture credits

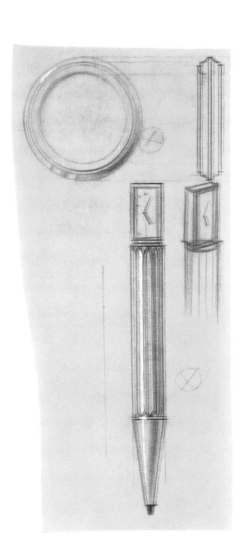

PRECEDING PAGES: Two **studies** for spherical inkwells and pens (circa 1930). Pencil, India ink, and gouache on tracing paper. Cartier Archives. THIS PAGE: Design for a **combination pen and watch** (circa 1930) in gold, fluted silver, and black lacquer. Pencil and gouache on cardboard. Cartier Archives. FOLLOWING PAGE: **Production design** for a paper knife (1927) with a crocidolite handle, cherry tortoiseshell blade, and enameled band set with cabochon sapphires and emeralds. Pencil and gouache on tracing paper. Cartier Archives.